William Shakespeare:
The Romances

Twayne's English Authors Series

Arthur F. Kinney, Editor
University of Massachusetts, Amherst

TEAS 478

Geraint Wyn Davies as Pericles.

William Shakespeare: The Romances

By Elizabeth Bieman

University of Western Ontario

Twayne Publishers
A Division of G. K. Hall & Co. • *Boston*

William Shakespeare: The Romances
Elizabeth Bieman

Copyright 1990 by G. K. Hall & Co.
All rights reserved.
Published by Twayne Publishers
A division of G. K. Hall & Co.
70 Lincoln Street
Boston, Massachusetts 02111

Copyediting supervised by Barbara Sutton.
Book production by Janet Z. Reynolds.
Book design by Barbara Anderson.
Typeset in 11 pt. Garamond by Compositors Corp., Cedar Rapids, Iowa.

Printed on permanent/durable acid-free paper
and bound in the United States of America.

First published 1990.
10 9 8 7 6 5 4 3 2 1

Library of Congress Cataloging-in-Publication Data

Bieman, Elizabeth
         William Shakespeare : the romances / by Elizabeth Bieman.
             p.   cm. — (Twayne's English authors series ; TEAS 478)
         Includes bibliographical references.
         ISBN 0-8057-6995-1
         1. Shakespeare, William, 1564–1616—Tragicomedies.   I. Title.
     II. Series.
     PN2981.5.B54   1990
     822.3′3—dc20   89-26857
                                                              CIP

For my gracious daughters,
Cory and Kristin,
in memory of their grandmother, Grace

Contents

About the Author

Elizabeth Bieman is professor emeritus at the University of Western Ontario, from which she received her undergraduate and graduate degrees. She has published numerous articles—on Spenser, Marlowe, Shakespeare, Coleridge, Browning, and modern Canadian writers—most of which demonstrate her continuing concerns with Neoplatonism, biblical myth, and hermeneutic theory. The first six chapters of her recent book, *Plato Baptized: Towards the Interpretation of Spenser's Mimetic Fictions* (University of Toronto Press, 1988), form a useful introduction to most texts from Renaissance England, and especially to the Shakespeare of the Romances.

Editor's Note

The last plays of Shakespeare have often been given simplistic allegorical readings or overlooked in a body of work with more accessible comedies and tragedies, but this new study by Elizabeth Bieman shows in its comprehensive and often fresh readings how they are for Shakespeare a significant part of his drama. By first examining the romance tradition from earlier periods as Shakespeare's age came to know it, Bieman is able to place these late works in a contemporary context; by applying an understanding of the *puer* and the *senex* to them, she is able to shed new light on how even the minor characters are centrally related to the dramas in which they appear. By analyzing *Pericles* as "a skeletal paradigm of the unrealistic conventions of romance," *Cymbeline* as a fuller experiment that employs "every narrative and dramatic trick at Shakespeare's command," *The Winter's Tale* as "modifying the genre through realism," and *The Tempest* as a play that moves past realism into the workings of the human psyche, then as now, she demonstrates clearly the deep rather than the superficial linkages among Shakespeare's final major works for the stage. These readings, moreover, which see the romances as plays essentially about the family, also examine them in the light of new historicism, political rule, and family and sexual politics. This widely accessible study should greatly expand the interest and understanding of four plays that have been considerably underrated for too long.

Arthur F. Kinney

Preface

The four plays this book groups for deliberation under the name of the Romances have enough similarities to justify that name, and more than enough differences—from each other and from other romances—to call it into question. But other possible names can raise other questions. *Tragicomedy* fits the first three Romances but will encompass also such comedies as, perhaps, *Much Ado About Nothing* and, certainly, *Measure for Measure*. *Tragicomedy* fits *The Tempest* only if we stretch the tale Prospero tells Miranda back into that undelineated "dark . . . abysm of time" that precedes the tightly unified action on the island stage. *The final plays,* another name they often bear, is inaccurate. *Henry VIII* and *The Two Noble Kinsmen* had yet to be written when Shakespeare, with Prospero, "retired."

Romance, too, raises problems, but it more than compensates. Pointing us to the quest of a "hero"—whether active, accidental, or providential—for a prize that transmutes itself, at length, into the gold of self-knowledge, the word *romance* provides the key I find best for unlocking these strange texts. Each play, read as quest and questioning, subjects a male protagonist (Pericles, Leontes, Posthumus, Prospero) to the processes that transform the masculine psyche into something rich and strange—richer and stranger than the subject could possibly foresee before events bring his buried or violated inner "virgin" into harmonious conjunction with his archetypal masculinity in his brave new world.

The language in the previous sentence points past the narrative substance of romance to the connected mysteries of Renaissance alchemy and twentieth-century depth psychology. The introductory chapter of this book will elaborate on these connections and on other matters in the literature, philosophy, and theology of Shakespeare's time that give contexts for understanding the transformative force of the Romances. Attention will also turn to questions arising from feminist theory. What happens to women when they play the roles a patriarchal society assigns to them? Questions from literary and dramatic theory will also arise. What happens when a poet, a playwright, a director, an actor, "imitates" life? What happens when an audience a critic, a reader, interprets mimetic art? The questions will turn back into the plays and point to the balancing reunion in the psyche of those forces that society splits off into "masculine" and "feminine" and to the "participation" in dramatic art that offers a means (by no means coercively certain) of transforming consciousness. Each of the four successive chapters examines a play.

Some of the problematic issues arising in the first play, *Pericles,* will be clarified by the introductory material. Thinking alchemically, we shall find that the brothel scenes so hated by the Victorians figure forth the baseness of a human substance potentially golden. Thinking in post-Jungian terms, we shall find continuities between the hero as boyish idealist and the hero as shaggy, saturnine old man. This play's Greek title and its final setting in the temple of the goddess Diana mark it with the ancient pagan exoticism typical of one stream of Renaissance romance. The subsequent Romances, less remote and irrelevant, we shall see moving by stages closer to the audiences' home territory. One is set in ancient Britain, one in the "Bohemia" and "Sicilia" of Christian Europe, and one ultimately leaves the island between Milan and Tunis for the unbounded immediacy of the great "Globe" itself.

As in *Pericles,* we find in *Cymbeline* a questing male hero, Posthumus, whose story is illuminated by depth psychology. Unlike *Pericles,* this play gives us a heroine who is more than an object or an agent in the hero's transformation. Imogen herself is subject to transformation. We shall also note in *Cymbeline* one of the strangest, most frenetic plots ever to come from Shakespeare's pen. It romps down several intertwined paths taken from chronicle, pastoral, folktale, and worldly prose fiction to an ending poised in the mythic triumph of "such a peace" as "never was." The final serenity will prevail only moments in our imaginations: the cynicism of the Iachimo plot cuts so deeply that we shall not forget for long the evils inevitable in the worlds we know as individuals.

The Winter's Tale begins with the seedy, realistic suspicions of Leontes, which, like those of Posthumus, lead to outrageous injustice against the innocent. Like *Cymbeline,* it eventually leads us into a pastoral world where transforming energies prevail. Like both of its predecessors, this tale involves a woman's innocence threatened yet unshaken; unlike them it initially splits feminine chastity from female power, parceling the virtues out separately to Hermione and Paulina. Although it unites both virtues in Perdita, when it re-empowers a transformed Leontes it leaves all under his patriarchal control. We shall locate some hope in Florizel but must recognize that he might come to resemble the fathers of these plays as he ages in their kind of world. Whatever our hopes for the new generation, Shakespeare focuses on their elders at the close of this, and the next, play.

The Tempest recapitulates the issues of sin and endangered innocence raised in the other three, but it brings them much closer than those ever do to Jacobean audience and postmodern readers. Prospero's magic erodes all boundaries between stagecraft and life, fiction and fact, outer and inner dimensions of experience. As the play funnels ever deeper into Prospero's troubled, disempowered humanity, it takes us with him. Prospero's theurgy, used as benignly within the fiction as Shakespeare has been using his dramaturgy to renew those susceptible to good influence, must be abandoned lest it suffer corruption through the internal darkness represented by Caliban. The epilogue, seeking relief from the internal danger the disempowered magician acknowledges, speaks for every audience and reader drawn into full participation by Shakespeare's soon-to-be-abandoned power.

Because the four chapters replay the four Romances in interpreting them, and each chapter, like each play, is directed toward a further, and different, performance in the theater of each reader's imagination, I attempt no full conclusion in the brief Afterword. Each new performance must be granted its autonomy.

Elizabeth Bieman

University of Western Ontario

Acknowledgments

Like every interpreter of Shakespeare, I owe debts to the countless other interpreters whose work I have read over the decades. Beside that more distant majority who must remain unspecified, I am conscious of debts immediate and direct.

First, I acknowledge my own considerable gains when I explored the four Romances in the fall term of 1987 with fifteen lively graduate students. Many of the insights arising in that seminar reappear in these pages. To my regret, many others of worth and sophistication have fallen outside the scope of a book of this length. I think also, here, of those students in a twenty-year succession of honors Shakespeare classes who have expanded my understanding by their enthusiasms, their probing questions, and their alternative readings.

Next, I thank that coterie of post-Jungian analysts—especially James Hillman, Marie-Louise von Franz, and Marion Woodman—whose texts have enabled one without formal credentials in their discipline to follow the signs Shakespeare inscribed in such phrases as "boy eternal" (*Winter's Tale,* 1.2.65) and in the striking virginal figures of these Romances.

Thanks, too, to Ross Woodman, Cory Bieman Davies, and Graeme Bieman, each of whom has read and commented on some part of the manuscript. Even more helpful have been the conversations in which each has served me as sounding board. I thank Arthur Kinney, the series editor, for his invaluable editorial skills, and most especially for initiating what has proved to be such a joyful task for me. Similarly, I thank Lewis De Simone and Barbara Sutton, editors at Twayne Publishers, for their skills and courtesies.

In successive years on this project, I have enjoyed research assistance from Allison Marlow and Jan Plug through the Work / Study Bursary Program of the Ontario government. To these young scholars I am truly grateful. Further support for research and preparation of the manuscript has been provided through the office of the dean of arts at the University of Western Ontario from funds supplied by the Social Sciences and Humanities Research Council of Canada.

The facilities of the D. B. Weldon Library at the University of Western Ontario have proved, as usual, to meet most of the needs of a busy Renaissance scholar. I am particularly grateful for the study space I have enjoyed during the period of writing.

I thank my colleague, Alan Somerset, and Lisa Brant, archivist of the Stratford Festival (Stratford, Ontario), and particularly Geraint Wyn Davies, for help in connection with the frontispiece.

Chronology of the Romances

The dates are approximate and represent the time during which the texts probably were given their extant shape. Except for *Pericles* (which was registered for publication the year before the Quarto of 1609), the dates bear no relationship to first publication. (The other three Romances were first printed in the Folio of 1623.)

1608–1609	*Pericles*
1608–1611	*Cymbeline*
1611	*The Winter's Tale*
1611	*The Tempest*

It is worth noting that the last of the great tragedies, *Coriolanus*, is roughly contemporaneous with *Pericles* and that after his retirement to Stratford Shakespeare wrote *Henry VIII* (1613) and collaborated with John Fletcher (and perhaps Sir Francis Beaumont) on *The Two Noble Kinsmen* (1613–1616).

Chapter One

"Such provision in mine Art":
Contexts for Interpretation

Pericles, Cymbeline, The Winter's Tale, and *The Tempest* have grouped themselves naturally in the minds of Shakespeare's audiences and readers for reasons more and less sound. We may dispose of the shakiest of these briefly; we shall be exploring the sounder interconnections among the Romances throughout this chapter, and indeed throughout the rest of the book.[1]

They are often called "the final plays"—although *Pericles,* because the text that has come down to us is badly distorted, was long excluded from the grouping. The epilogue to the latest, *The Tempest,* has often been read, sentimentally yet with textual foundation, as Shakespeare's personal farewell to his art. Yet the playwright-magician was not quite through with his calling when he stilled the strangely personal voice of Prospero. After he returned to his birthplace, Stratford, from the London stage, he wrote *Henry VIII* and collaborated with Fletcher on *The Two Noble Kinsmen.*

That error settled, we may safely recognize that "the final plays," written between 1607 and 1611, survey all that has gone before them. They move beyond the history plays, English and Roman, beyond the romantic comedies of young love, beyond the "problem plays," beyond the great tragedies, into their own distinctly Shakespearean genre, the tragicomic romance.

In the improbable fictive worlds these plays present, the pressures of actual politics and history may seem remote, but the right management of social and national issues is of central thematic concern in each, and the history of Shakespeare's own time is arguably a shaping factor in the imaginative conception of each.[2] Pairs of young lovers occupy center stage during some part of each play, but relationships between parental figures and their children of marriageable age are of at least as much significance to plot and theme as the actual romantic pairings. At the outset in each, tragic or potentially tragic elements unfold—lusts, jealousies, murderous intrigues—but these are deflected from consciousness, resolved, or redeemed as the actions press toward an ending happier than is plausible, or even perhaps possible, in life and more realistic fictions. Certain factors that give rise in the earlier "problem plays" to their label—steamy sexual corruption, "good" characters acting in thoroughly unadmirable ways, heroes who seem unworthy of the healing, chaste, or virginal women with whom they are paired—emerge again in the Romances, only to be subsumed, if not forgotten, in the overarching resolutions of their endings.

Transformations of many sorts, transformations that redeem and resurrect, restoring harmony in the social order and the souls of the protagonists, mark the final actions of these otherwise very different plays. "All's well that ends well" and "As you like it"—the proverbially flavored titles of two earlier comedies—characterize the effects of each romance and the embracing comic pattern that together they complete in the Shakespearean canon.

Romance

The motif of transformation or metamorphosis, often from deathlike states to new life, prevails as constant in the otherwise protean literary genre, romance. To consider the debt Shakespeare owes here to tradition, and the innovations that make the Romances peculiarly his, and thus new, we need to glance at what we have in mind when we use the term *romance*—characteristics established by texts from earlier centuries.

We think first of plot or story, usually childlike stories, strange and marvelous, in which, as in fairy tales, the unexpected is more to be expected than the commonplace. The plots of romance are often linear, operating more by laws of accretion and juxtaposition than by the interconnections of common sense or reason. The very irrationality of romance works its own magic. It calls the interpretive function of listener, reader, or audience more vigorously into play than the realism of such stories as seem to offer more obvious and open meanings. Romance invites us to ponder the imponderable, to erect meanings of our own on its slippery foundations by interpreting events and characters in a variety of allegorical ways. Of the plays with which this book is concerned, *The Tempest* has probably been submitted most often to this sort of reading because of the obvious subhuman and supernatural elements we find in Caliban and Ariel. But all four Romances invite some degree of allegorical reading, as we shall see in the chapters to come. When I speak of allegorical texts and allegorical readings in reference to Shakespeare, I think of the polyvalent allegory characteristic of medieval and Renaissance writers like Dante and Spenser and of the most flexible readings of such texts. I do not mean to suggest anything like the rigid imposition of a single meaning onto a series of metaphors (often in the interest of some dogma) that has given "allegory" a deservedly bad name ever since the Romantics.

We might think next of character. Characters in the stories of most romances are very bad or very good, like characters in fairy tales and legends. We love to hate the villains and identify with the good. As readers of romance, we are like children who experience growth by self-definition as we identify with the good younger brothers and sisters who in fairy tales surmount the trials imposed upon them by hateful stepmother—witches, harsh older siblings, cruel giants, and evil magicians.

Shakespeare's Romances, of course, move far beyond such schematic simplicity. But they are peopled by extremes: by villains and rascals, many unredeemable, such as Antiochus in *Pericles,* the Queen and Cloten in *Cymbeline,* Autolycus in *The Winter's Tale,* and Antonio in *The Tempest;* and by powerfully innocent (usually virginal) characters like Marina, Imogen, Hermione, and Miranda, and—to provide balance in age and gender—Helicanus and Simonides, the faithful Pisanio, and Gonzalo. The central male characters in these plays, however, are as morally ambivalent as most of humanity. Pericles is oddly fugitive, as well as patient, in the face of evil and needs rescuing from a depression deep enough to deserve the name of sloth, if not of despair, to any archaically moralizing allegorist. Posthumus behaves outrageously toward his bride, and, if we seek to excuse him, we must search hard for justification beyond the villainy of Iachimo to whom he yields too easily. Leontes' jealousy is as irrational as Othello's, less excusable in the absence of an Iago, and it arises in circumstances that do not distance him, as Othello is distanced, from the grounds of social and personal confidence. Prospero wields his redemptive magic with a harshness that brings us, through Miranda and Ariel, to question seriously his motives, if not his actions.

Some of the origins of romance as a genre have already been suggested: fairy tales, folktales, and legends. The genre was much elaborated and extended during the Middle Ages in the long narrative poems that bear its name. Medieval romance contributed significantly to English romantic epics, like Sidney's *Arcadia* and Spenser's *Faerie Queene;* but the romances closest in type to Shakespeare's final plays are neither Sidney's nor Spenser's, those closest in time and literary place, nor the slightly more distant Arthurian cycles and other romantic sagas of northern Europe. They are romances from the late Greek civilization of North Africa, newly translated and popular in Renaissance Europe. The *Aethiopica* by Heliodorus, "Englished" in Shakespeare's time by Thomas Underdowne, provides an example.

The multiple plots of the *Aethiopica* follow a pair of lovers, Theagenes and Chariclea, both brave and good. The young man is marked by extraordinary physical as well as moral courage and the lady by a goddesslike virginal purity. They have been separated long from their homes in Greece and Ethiopia. Their paths cross and recross as they undergo, usually separately but occasionally together, various captivities, escapes, journeys, and encounters with fearsome magic (a speaking corpse, for example). Each meets shadowy opposites—he in the rapacious captors and monsters he must escape or quell, she in women wanton or incestuous. Chariclea's purity protects her on many occasions, including once when she has been falsely accused, tried, and condemned to execution by fire. The flames raging about her do her no more harm than those of Nebuchadnezzar's furnace did to the faithful three of Israel in a late Old Testament romance (Daniel 3:8–30).[3] Supernatural powers pervade their stories; under trial the young lovers call upon the gods for aid, and sometimes the narrator ascribes their improbable escapes to destiny. By the time of the wildly complicated final episodes, Theagenes and Chariclea have been piously but secretly married; have adopted the ancient biblical and folktale ruse of passing as brother and sister before strangers; have been captured and brought to the court of the king of Ethiopea. There Chariclea is revealed to be his long-lost daughter, her identity confirmed by a faithful old courtier, Sisimithres, and by various physical signs. Her beloved remains under sentence of death, even as he triumphs through tests of his physical and moral strength by a Goliath-like opponent and a rampaging bull. Eventually the revered Sisimithres convinces the king that the gods themselves have contributed to the miraculous safety of Theagenes to show that they do not wish the sacrifice of this hero. At the close all threads of the plot are revealed and properly tied, all familial and international harmony restored, in an atmosphere of piety and love.

Such was this one analogue to Shakespeare's Romances. Whether he knew it directly is of little consequence, although he probably did. The intertextual field of Renaissance romance abounds in the elements we could isolate from the *Aethiopica* to relate to counterparts in Shakespeare. The purity and strength of Marina, Imogen, and Hermione (and of Miranda, although she is spared the extremities of trial) follow the pure strength of countless heroines like Chariclea; the staunch virtues of Helicanus, Pisanio, Camillo, and Gonzalo reflect those of many like Sisimithres. The wildly improbable close of *Cymbeline* matches more breathless finales than that of the *Aethiopica*.

But Shakespeare did not follow his models slavishly. His aging or aged characters are far more prominent than those in the earlier examples. Romance before him was a genre of youth and spring. But Pericles, Cymbeline, Leontes, and Prospero know their winters, and *The Winter's Tale* bears the very name of age and cold. Most important, the young men in Shakespeare's Romances are either deficient in the virtues Theagenes exemplifies, or, like

Ferdinand and Florizel, they play a relatively minor role. Florizel is a stronger character than Ferdinand, but he is overshadowed by Leontes. It is the women, Marina, Imogen, Hermione, and Perdita, we find representing the extremes of virtue; Pericles is strangely passive, Posthumus and Leontes inexplicably untrusting and unjust. To have seen Theagenes, and his heroic young peers in earlier romances, is to be prepared to recognize some very strange differences when we turn to Shakespeare's individual plays. Virtue, in his central male protagonists, comes only with wisdom, after prolonged trials inflicted and endured.

Ritual

The dominance of plot and action in the Romances, however fleshed out by Shakespeare's vivid characterization and dialogue, heightens in them the effect of ritual, which lies at the very root of all theater. Ritual depends on, and supports, the conviction that actions performed in the right way, by the right people, in the right spirit, can bring about transformation. Practice and conviction are interdependent. Many anthropologists believe that enactment is prior to story, that ritual produces the faith recapitulated in myth more often than it reflects such prior faith. In later chapters we shall look at examples of good and evil rituals within the plays. But here I am concerned with how these plays as wholes participate to an unusual degree in effects we are more likely to identify with religious ritual than with theater.

Whether we think of the pagan rituals of the Mediterranean world, which are revived so often in the late Greek romances, and in Shakespeare's, or think of the Christian rituals with which Shakespeare's audiences and modern readers are more directly familiar, we can say that religious rituals posit the existence of supernatural forces, bring them into play, and interact with them, and that, at least theoretically, they enable participants to experience directly the saving divine processes remembered and magically invoked by ritual enactment.

The consciousness supporting primitive ritual, insofar as it can be reconstructed, reveals a pattern that moves through chaos or disintegration—figured mythically and dramatically in battles, monsters, wanderings at sea, disorders, and injustices of many sorts—to transformative reorderings of persons, events, and societies. The chaos endured is not merely the temporal preliminary to restoration but is mysteriously, almost we sense causally, basic to it. Before something can be reformed or transformed, it must be rendered formless. Our current awareness of such structures of consciousness has been sharpened by work like that of Mircea Eliade in comparative religion, but

Shakespeare demonstrates in the structures and finer language of most of his plays that Renaissance thinking manifested the same timeless patterns.[4] Such patterns still inform the rituals of most evolved psychological disciplines and religions. The mystic goes through a purging of negative elements of the self, and a dark night of the soul, before the time of blissful re-formation in union with the divine. The alchemist makes his elements dissolve and putrefy before the transformed product—the gold, the vital elixir, or the higher spiritual consciousness in the worker—can emerge. The Christian must have the old Adam dissolved in the waters of baptism and must assimilate the divine in the torn body and blood of the eucharistic elements before the soul can be saved, reborn as re-formed into the wholeness intended at creation but never enjoyed by the fallen creature without the gifts of supernatural grace available through the sacraments.

Within the action of these four ritualistic Romances healers restore life, gods speak, magicians work good magic to change things and persons, over whom, like the alchemist, they have power. But as readers and audience, we should look beyond the mere fictions. We should observe our own reactions in the theater of performance and response; we should recognize the effects of these theatrical rituals on our own representatively human spirits.

I recall the response of one student, a quite typical and self-contained young man although clearly an unusually sensitive reader. He caught me on the way into class one day to tell me that he had read *Pericles* in one sitting the night before, had been caught up in astonishment, and still felt his feet hovering above the prosaic earth. Oblivious to the patent fictionality of *Pericles'* world of coincidence, repetition, and miracle, he was responding to the pattern of triumph and restoration traced in the play's unfolding. He felt marvelous. He was not so much, with Coleridge, willing the suspension of disbelief as simply responding with heart and gut to the powers of healing transformation the play represents. The effect had lasted at least twelve overnight hours.

I recall, too, young children responding even less self-consciously to these plays. Children rarely notice the complexities of sexual innuendo, and they rarely question magic and miracle. Once I saw a fine performance of *The Tempest* at Stratford, Ontario, with my daughter and her ten-year-old classmates. I was rapt above my otherwise probable adult reactions to the masque scenes by participating in the sharp, hushed gasps of wonder around me when Ariel produced a banquet from nowhere in the "inexplicable splendor of white and gold."[5] My memories of the more complex reactions of my daughters to *The Winter's Tale*, even younger then at eight and five, are still vivid. On the long drive home from a matinee, I was eavesdropping on the conversation in the back seat.

The younger speaks first: "I don't know why that king was so mean to the queen. She wasn't doing anything wrong. She was just being friendly, and he asked her to be friendly."

"That's right. But he thought she was being too friendly. I was really mad at him too. He was stupid. I wonder why she was so nice to him at the end. I wouldn't have been."

"Well," said the little one, "I guess it was to make them both feel better."

I still marvel a little at the wisdom of babes, but I realize it was a wisdom that the ritual of that performance had communicated to one not yet old enough to be, like Dr. Johnson, hypercritical of "absurdity of conduct" in a romance.[6] Her sister was, like most of us by a certain age, taking expectations of a commonsensical sort into the theater: common sense got in the way of her participating fully in the ritual of an innocent who suffers, forgives, and eventually redeems a victimizer. But if we meet them with a childlike acceptance, the Romances will make us all feel better, at least for a time.

Shakespeare is, of course, not a childish playwright, whatever his invitations to childlike responses. Entwined with the potent details of skeletal plot, he offers intricacies of character and language that give us second and third thoughts, even if we have recovered the childlike in our initial responses. He wears his learning lightly in the Romances but often demonstrates his awareness of certain ancient traditions that contributed to the various Renaissance languages of transformation. To some of these I now turn.

Transformation: Magic, Alchemy, Miracle

White and black magic, alchemy, and miracle working often take the foreground in the plots of the Romances. Cerimon, the good physician, restores Thaisa, Pericles' queen, to life after her apparent death at sea; Imogen's wicked stepmother, Cymbeline's queen, poisons her with a magic potion, rendering her apparently lifeless; Paulina performs the apparent miracle of restoring Hermione to life at the close of *The Winter's Tale;* Prospero controls his island world by magic so successfully that he restores himself to the life of political power he once enjoyed. Something of ritual effect evolves through each of these fictions of magic: Shakespeare seems to be celebrating a supernatural power of restoration, whatever its name.

Let us look now briefly at the roots of these traditions of magic and alchemy, which, however much in flux in Shakespeare's time, retained some of their old power for the Renaissance imagination.

Belief in, and practice of, what we now call magic predates all written human records. In the Hellenistic Mediterranean culture reflected in the Greek romances, it was strong and influential. Basically, the magic worker manipulates material substances, and sounds and words, to bring about changes of a desired sort in material, psychological, or spiritual areas. The magician (he is traditionally male, female "magicians" usually bearing the less honored name of "witch") sees himself as wielding power over both the agencies of change and the substances or persons changed. Whether he is employing the spirits of the elements (like Ariel and, less obviously, Caliban) or enlisting higher supernatural daemons as his helpers, his is the control. In polytheistic cultures the magician might serve one god or other supernatural being to gain the god's power for his own control over the lower world or over the devotees of another god. But in biblical cultures, from the time of Saul and the Witch of Endor forward, magic has always been suspect.[7] In relation to the biblical God, the sole true and good supernatural power, the human creature must always be properly subservient. When God gives a human subject power, it is always as his own agent: prophets channel his messages, priests perform his powerful rituals, kings rule as his regents over nations. By the time of the Renaissance, orthodox thinkers understood "Christian magic" to be a contradiction in terms. Any power that a magician might claim for himself must, it was thought, stem from God's adversary, Satan, or from another demon. The plot of Marlowe's *Doctor Faustus* illustrates such orthodox attitudes (not necessarily those of Marlowe). But among occultists who considered themselves Christian, some still believed cautiously in white magic as a discipline for working good.

The foundations for such belief were very old. Even in the ancient world lines were drawn quite clearly between an exalted spiritual magic consistent with pagan piety, then termed *theurgeia,* and a debased magic, *goeteia,* by which the magician worked changes to satisfy his own appetite and ambition.

Iamblichus, a devout Neoplatonic philosopher of the fourth century, explains in his *On the Mysteries of the Egyptians, Assyrians, and Chaldeans* that the rituals employed by the devout to bring down the power of the gods or to work the *anagoge,* the elevation, of the practitioner's spirit are lawful and favored in the sight of the divine. The gods have given knowledge of these techniques so that they themselves may be the better understood, experienced, and served. Iamblichus's text provides a grounding for our understanding of magic in the Romances. It highlights the issues that made Christians in the Renaissance wary of the very word *magic,* but it provides arguments that the practitioners of theurgic magic in the Renaissance (like Marsilio Ficino in Italy, and Dr. John Dee in Elizabethan England) found strong enough to support their daring in the face of powerful, and punitive, orthodoxy.[8]

The theurgic practitioners of the ancient world were often conscious of their rivalry with the priests of the Christian church, just as in Old Testament stories Pharaoh's magicians and the "prophets of Baal" stood as rivals to God's priest, Aaron, and his prophet, Elijah (Exod. 7; 1 Kings 18). In Iamblichus's day, the Christian religion was surging to popularity throughout the Mediterranean world, not least because its impressive rituals enabled even the lowly and illiterate to participate in the divine power. The Neoplatonic philosopher Plotinus had taught an austere intellectual and spiritual discipline that depended on dialectic and meditation for its elevating effects, but his followers recognized the need to develop more tangible, and hence magical, techniques if they were to engage the common people.

Among the rituals of theurgic magic Iamblichus describes are those in which the priest appears, dramatically, to bring a statute to life (pertinent, obviously, to the many apparent resurrections of the Romances) and others in which music of the precise harmonies necessary for participating in the higher harmonies of the universe is played to transform the consciousness of the practitioner. We can see that the imaginative systems Iamblichus describes, typical of many in the ancient world, are paralleled, with only slight differences, in Shakespeare's imaginative worlds. There chaos, figured frequently in tempest-tossed seas and thundering storms, must be endured before the harmonies of renewal, reconciliation, and social concord can be enjoyed. In Shakespeare music is usually the outward sign of such desirable states.

Alchemy, the progenitor of both modern chemistry and certain psychological techniques for transformation of the self, can properly be described as a highly learned magical discipline. Like any magician, the alchemist works with physical substances, language being understood here as itself substantial, since the movement of the organs of speech, of air, and (in writing) the elements of hand, ink, and paper, are necessary to it. Like the goetic magician, the alchemist may seek personal wealth and satisfaction through his work; like the theurgist, the higher sort of alchemist may understand his work as a means to transform himself spiritually.

By Shakespeare's time, most literal claims of the alchemists to make gold and the elixir of life were disbelieved, although the alchemists' knowledge of drugs and potions was not dismissed. What escaped literal acceptance lived on as metaphor. To the poetic imagination, alchemy meant transformation; Donne found its language effective in writing of the marvels of love. Theater, itself so mysteriously an agency of transformation through survivals of ritual, came to think of itself frequently through the metaphors of magic and alchemy.[9] The very presence in Renaissance drama, and particularly in the Romances, of so many wonder-workers gives strong representation to the conviction that drama does matter, that it can change persons and events—in the theater and beyond.

Charles Nicholl, in *The Chemical Theatre*, says this of alchemy in Shakespeare's time: "The play, as dream made visible, is perhaps not so far from that 'spiritual fixt thing' that the alchemist sought to witness in the theatre of his vessel. . . . What we see revealed . . . is something hidden inside ourselves." He points, in this conclusion, to ideas of psychological transformation we can find in Jungian psychology.[10] But before proceeding to that context, I must briefly define, in relation to these plays, the differences between "magic" and "miracle" and speak of one miracle of transformation familiar to Shakespeare's contemporaries under the metaphor of "baptism."

Miracle can be irreverently defined as the magic of the religion that a given miracle-monger subscribes to, but to define it that way is to miss an important point. Magic's effects (except in the ambivalent area of theurgic magic) are attributed to the power of the magician. Miracle's effects, on the other hand, are attributed to the power of the divine, whether that is vested in an Olympian deity, in the Bible's God (often as mediated through the Virgin Mary or a saint), or even in what Perdita calls "great creating nature."[11] Thus a more serviceable definition of a miracle for discussing plays written for Christian audiences in a Christian period would be "a manifestation of the transformative power of God in either physical or spiritual events." Because the biblical God's power is infinite (unlike that of one god among the many on Olympus) and because human expectations and understandings are limited, those "miracles" of transformation that do occur are both surprising and infinitely meaningful.

By this definition, miracle need not be thought to transgress the hidden laws of the physical universe (could those be understood), but it must seem to transgress the limits to some given human situation or expectation. The great miracles of these final plays, we shall see, are not so much instances of change and reversal in a physical state (the changes that the lower forms of magic effect) as they are the showings forth of the divine pattern that will transform those who really come to see it. That pattern has been implied but not identified in the discussion of ritual.

Baptism, the Sacred Banquet, and
Psychological Transformation

The central rituals of the Christian religion, whatever the sect or church, are baptism and the communal banquet. Both provide models for many of the episodes in Shakespeare's Romances. The safe and renovating passages through storms at sea we find in *Pericles, Winter's Tale,* and *The Tempest* are like baptisms. *Cymbeline* uses a strange ritual, almost a parodic baptism, as a turning point: Imogen anoints herself with blood, not water, and thereafter sees herself in her world quite differently. The conviviality at the table of the good King Simonides in *Pericles,* the sheep-shearing feast in *The Winter's Tale,* and the masque of judgment and the wedding masque in *The Tempest* are allegorically like the Mass, the Eucharist, the Lord's Supper.

That holy meal may vary in name, in ritual detail, and in doctrinal explanation, but it always involves the "partaking" of common elements representing, and re-presenting, the body and blood of the God who allowed Himself to be broken so that broken men and women could enjoy wholeness. I shall have more to say about "partaking" and "representation" later when I am talking about the concept of "imitation" (mimesis), but for now I point only to the reciprocal nature of the ritual enactment and to its transformative effect.

Baptism, the ritual washing away of "sins," was the only other of the seven medieval sacraments to be retained in the reformed churches. It seems initially to be simpler to interpret as a symbol of transformation than the ritual meal. In oversimplified conservative doctrine, it is understood to transform the guilty creature (often an infant) to one washed clean of sin, as Jesus himself was washed by the Baptist in Jordan. The paradoxes here are obvious. How has an infant "sinned," except as a descendant of the sinners in Eden? And if that is the explanation, how can "sin" be inherited? How had Jesus sinned? Even if, metaphorically, he is the second Adam, he is that in part because he is the first man since Adam to be born free of sin. To unravel such paradoxes theologians were driven to far more speculation, intrication, and complication than we can recall here. But one metaphoric understanding of baptism, current in Shakespeare's time, will help.[12]

William Perkins, a theologian contemporary with Shakespeare whose tradition reaches back through Calvin and Augustine to Paul, speaks of spiritual baptism as the renewal of understanding that can be experienced repeatedly through the lifetime of each ritually baptized Christian. The unrepeatable ritual that has incorporated the self into Christ in an atemporal mutuality makes Christ available as "inner teacher," as guide in all further moments of the kind of knowing we can call "personal"—flashes of understanding when the moment's, or a lifetime's, perplexities are clarified by glimpses of a new and broader pattern. That pattern, for Perkins, is available in Scripture but only when it is properly interpreted. He presents his argument in the form of a dialogue.

A questioner, told that his baptism "seals . . . the mercies of God" by "convey[ing] Christ and all his benefits" to those who are "full of unbelief and doubting of them," and that Christ is the "inner Teacher," says: "We are all baptized. Belike then we shall all understand scripture." Not so, alas, he is told. "Very few there be that are taught and feel their ingrafting into Christ, their justification, their inward dying unto sin and living unto righteousness, which is the meaning of their baptism." Without the "feeling" that confirms, a personal kind of knowing, the pattern of life in Scripture is "shut up" "though Peter, Paul or Christ himself did expound it." There is clearly a difference between the intellectual and doctrinal knowledge that comes through having something "expounded" to us and the "feeling" knowing that comes through deep personal experience. This deeper kind of knowing is what Perkins calls the "meaning of . . . baptism."[13]

The scriptural basis for this understanding of baptism is found in the story of Paul's conversion in Acts 9, wherein "something like scales" falls from the apostle's eyes before he is ritually baptized. Paul normally thereafter speaks of, and draws from, his personal knowing in terms of renewal and salvation. He explains that he himself has not come so much "to baptize" as to "preach the cross" (1 Cor. 1:17–18). In present terminology, he has not come, like John the Baptist, to perform ritual ablutions but to lead his hearers to experience the indwelling Christ as he himself now does. Paul understands that his mission is to lead others to spiritual or metaphoric baptism, to a new personal knowing of Christ, who will henceforth dwell within the knower.

To clarify further, we need to consider what the New Testament writers mean by the word *hamartia*, usually translated as "sin." The Greek originally meant "missing the mark," as an archer or runner might do. Such failure calls not for a cleansing from defilement or guilt but for better aim. Shakespeare uses this metaphor in *King Lear*. When Kent tells the tyrannically foolish old king, "See better, Lear, and let me still remain / The true blank of thine eye," he seeks to overcome the king's *hamartia* by offering him a clearer sight of the target's "blank"—the center of the pattern of his aging life.[14]

When we understand sin in this way, we see that the once-and-for-all-time ritual of baptism is merely the foundational step in a Christian's life process. Thereafter, the Christ, ritually incorporated, can either be ignored in the dark recesses of the self or can light up each important new experience as "inner Teacher." As light and Logos (pattern)—both scriptural ways of speaking of Christ (John 1:1–5)—he shows the true field of a life's circumstances and the true pattern it should develop. Each enlightening moment, each new awareness, Shakespeare's contemporaries could have understood as a "metaphoric baptism"; it could adjust the failing aim of the past by clarifying the goal anew.[15]

But for now I move on to a brief discussion of Renaissance psychology and then to more modern ways of thinking symbolically about changes in the patterns of life, using languages and methods developed by Freud, Jung, and their followers in psychological analysis.

Transformation in Psychological Analysis

The understanding of the human psyche or soul had changed relatively little from ancient times to the Renaissance. It was usually pictured in a three-part hierarchy that originated with Plato: the highest immaterial spirit, *nous,* which translates to intellect, reason, higher imagination, and so forth, is located in the head; the mid-soul, *psyche* or soul, a principle of life that combines and holds together spirit and body is associated with the trunk, heart, or sometimes the liver; and the lower soul, a chaos of appetites and vegetable functions, is located in the body, especially its lower regions. The virtue of head is reason, of the mid-soul courage, of the lower soul, temperance. The total psyche is in healthy harmony when *nous,* in the aspect of reason, controls the lower parts. The psyche of each microcosmic individual images the macrocosm, the pattern of the universe, *nous* corresponding to the level of the divine; soul corresponding to the state or body politic; the body corresponding to the world of matter and subject to evil influences that would trap it there.

Subsequent thinkers adjusted Plato's scheme without abandoning it. Aristotle taught an ethics of the golden mean, seeing each of many virtues as a mean between two related vices—courage, for instance, coming between cowardice and rashness. It remained the function of *nous,* through reason, to choose virtuous actions. Plotinus taught philosophical exercises to refine and strengthen *nous,* to enable the adept to see the pattern of Oneness in the universe and, perhaps, to experience mystical union with the divine One. Augustine, combining biblical thinking with Greek, associated will, the agency of choice, with the mid-soul, under reason. When proper hierarchy was overturned, the passions or appetites of the lower soul overpowered a reason weakened by the Fall in Eden in shaping the will's choices. Inherited "original" sin was thus augmented by individual sin. This complex of theories prevailed in Shakespeare's time, and long thereafter—with, of course, continual adjustments.[16]

Sigmund Freud, almost a century ago, broke through to the understanding that those sick or troubled in psyche can be helped by techniques leading to the recovery of submerged memories of childhood.[17] These, set beside the circumstances of the present and near past, can enlighten current difficulties by pointing out the relationship between past and present. Through understanding parallels between the child and the man (early analysts thought in masculine terms, even when treating women), the psyche under treatment could often be "healed"—made whole by seeing life whole, in a larger patterned field, even if present circumstances must remain unchanged.[18]

Freud's understanding of the importance of memory to human life was not totally new. The Moses to whom he as a Jew turned now and again in his ponderings had himself (according to the tradition by which he had "written" the early books of the Bible) transformed Israel's memories of God's saving power into the poetry of Exodus 15. Whenever the people heard the "song of Moses," they would remember God's actions and own Him Lord "for ever and ever." Augustine had given memory a central place in his philosophy. John Donne, writing in 1611, within a year of *The Tempest*'s first performance, had recalled God's giving of the song to Moses for the people "because He knew they would let fall / The Law, the Prophets, and the History, / But keep the song still in their memory."[19] All these, like the later romantics, knew that to "look before and after" was the mark of true human life.[20] But it was Freud's radical advance to understand that the recovery of buried memories, those of which we are unconscious or barely conscious, is important for the full development of the adult psyche—for the full recognition of the relation of the individual to family and to the cultural environment.

Carl Gustav Jung, a student of Freud and founder of a rival school, moved far from Freud's usual focuses—those that located the roots of adult psychic turmoil in the sexual trauma of early childhood. Like Freud, Jung took the dreams of his clients seriously, but he interpreted their symbols more flexibly and multivalently than his predecessor, whom he accused of turning broadly significant symbols into oversimplified signs of repressed sexual experience. (In other words, Jung treats dreams as metaphor or as multivalent allegories, whereas Freud treats them as univalent, or "naive," allegories.) Jung defines his differences from Freud, first, by seeing the unconscious not as a demonic refuse heap of repressed sexual memories but as "a thing of nature that is perfectly neutral," morally, aesthetically, and intellectually; and second, by seeing the spiritual dimensions of the human psyche as more than sublimations of motives originally sexual.[21] Because he values traditional religious symbols while acknowledging the emptiness of much traditional doctrine, Jung's thinking is more productive than Freud's when applied to the Romances— where pagan deities and rituals call for nonreductive interpretation. Like Renaissance thinkers, Jung seeks to achieve a wholeness that depends on integrating the sexual, social, and spiritual in the human soul.

Several Jungian insights into human experience prove useful to the interpreter of the Romances. They will be outlined as needed in connection with the individual plays, but a few are worth introducing here.

Jung's hypothesis of the "collective unconscious," a deep "layer" at which the individual psyche approaches the universal and touches there the "archetypes" (the symbolic figures that inhabit and shape traditional myths and stories), helps explain the effects of ritual, theater, and other imaginative literature on the participating audience or reader.[22] The traditional symbols of pagan and biblical religions can tap the depths of the collective unconscious through ritual and poetry.

Jung's understanding of "individuation," that process by which human potential comes to full development in the individual life, translates readily into the traditional language of the "quest" in romance. In older romances, the questing hero was a young man seeking to find and prove himself by meeting and surmounting perils, loving and winning the perfect lady, and achieving in the end the exalted position in the social order he has always felt to be his due. Shakespeare, like Jung, recognized that soul making is a lifelong matter: quests may last long past chronological youth. The heroes of his Romances are not always young when they acquire self-knowledge. Like a few heroes of older tales but at a later stage in life, they are forced to abandon their life of ideals (to come to know their "shadows," as Jung would put it) in coming to know their own depths. Jung's archetype of the *puer aeternus* (based on Dionysos and other divine youths of ancient myth) yields insights relating to the sometimes dangerous idealism of the heroes of the Romances. The elaboration of Jung's thinking on the *puer* by Marie-Louise von Franz and its extension into *senex* psychology by James Hillman will also inform later chapters.

The symbols of transformation in alchemy fascinated Jung, who saw each step on the way to individuation as a transformative event. If alchemy did not shape his theories of the "animus" and "anima," it at least confirmed them. Sexual symbolism is central to both: the elixir, the gold, or the breakthrough in the alchemist's consciousness always depended on the "marriage" of the male and the female in the alchemical vessel, and the psyche; the "self," the end of the process of individuation, emerges through the balancing union of "animus" and "anima," the symbolically masculine and symbolically feminine, in the soul.

In later chapters, writers from both the post-Freudian and the post-Jungian streams of analysis will contribute to the discussion of the women who are so all important in the Romances. The same predominance of women will lead to speculation on sexual politics in Shakespeare's time and our own and on Shakespeare's own responses and contributions to the ever-shifting history of sexual relationships.

Participation in Mimesis

Like many other thinkers through the centuries he saw as formative to the collective unconscious, Jung himself saw "participation" as essential to the individual. "Just as it is impossible to individuate without relatedness, so it is impossible to have real relationships without individuation. For otherwise illusion comes in continually and you don't know where you are."[23] Participation on an individual basis is helped by the vision of universal archetypal relationships we can gain through art, which effects "a return to the state of *participation mystique*" wherein the particular is experienced as universal.[24]

Erich Neumann, a Jungian, explains "participation mystique" as a process whereby "vital energy leaves the human form that was hitherto its highest embodiment" to render the outside world "psychic" to the eye of the artist and to unite it to him subjectively as symbol. Through such participation artist and art object descend "like a waterfall" into the unconscious—and, in that world of archetypes the particular work merges with the collective, the universal.[25] Neumann's development of Jung's thinking on participation stands near the modern end of a continuum of philosophical thinking that stretches back through Plato to Pythagoras. Residues of that past survive, transformed, even yet. To trace the thinking back can help us define our own.

In Plato's time the deep question of relationship between particular created things and the originating universal principle was phrased in terms of the Many and the One. Aristotle tells us in the *Metaphysics* that Plato gave a new name, *methexis* (participation), to the relationship between the created Many and the creative One, and that by that word Plato meant what the Pythagoreans meant by *mimesis* (imitation): "What that participation or the imitation . . . could be they left an open question," he adds, as a practical sort of thinker not unduly concerned.

But in his own *Poetics,* a theoretical discussion of Greek drama, Aristotle himself uses the term *imitation* in a way that suggests, paradoxically, both the separating of a mirroring process and a limited degree of participation. *Poesis* (making) he says is the "imitation of an action," a mirroring of life, yet he goes on to say that the audience of drama, distanced from the imitated action, undergoes the "purging" of powerful negative emotions. If dramatic art were fully separated from life it could have no genuine effect on the audience. Somehow the fiction must bridge the gap between audience and world. That bridging can take the name of "participatory mimesis"[26] or imaginative participation, but naming the mystery will not make it less mysterious.

Later, the Neoplatonists living at the time of the Greek romances gave "participation" a privileged place in their theories of the relationship between the One (Plotinus's God) and the Many. For them participation was a two-way process: the One creates the Many by participating in them through its outflowing and downflowing goodness; the Many reciprocally participate in the One through their aspiring love for the Source. In the eddying circuitry of loving and creative participation, all creation is potentially renewed and redeemed.

The same word in a modified form, "partake," expresses the mystery whereby the Christian worshipper receives the descending mercy of God and ascends in response to Him when he or she partakes in the communal meal. God's self is given and taken in order that the ritual enactment join together communicator and communicant. Such a mystic participation gives rise to the effects of banquets on stage, which remind us of more direct transformations through eating. When we take food into ourselves, it comes to participate in the part of the self that is body; so also the food we share at a social banquet and the food we are given at a sacred banquet ensures our participation in the social bodies of which we are members and enables the life sustained at first physically to participate in the divine body around and within us.

A question arises through the link between "participation" and "mimesis." If drama is an imitation of an action, if Shakespeare is imitating life in the Romances, why are these fictions so unrealistic, so unlifelike? Often this question is displaced, if not answered, by a shift of theoretical ground. Romances are, by definition, not realistic. But Aristotle must have been aware in speaking of the play of Oedipus that men do not meet sphinxes every day, that action need not be literally interpretable. When Freud finds something real in the Oedipus story, it is not that boys grow up to mistakenly marry their mothers, but that at some deep level of consciousness they dream of doing so. The actions of any romance invite us to look within ourselves for significances that may be sexual, social, or spiritual but are not literal. Like our more personal dreams, these Romances enable us to participate under the illusion of safe distance in the universal cycles that undergird us and unfold in our individual stories.[27]

Chapter Two

"Thank the holy gods as loud as thunder threatens us": *Pericles*

The probable order in which the Romances were written puts *Pericles* first; many points of logic support chronological order for this book. The structural and stylistic problems in this play that sent earlier generations in search of a Shakespearean collaborator appear less serious when they follow directly after the introductory discussions on ritual and transformation. In its own right, *Pericles* serves effectively to introduce the series. Its sparseness exposes the motif of spiritual purity under threat (established here graphically by Marina in the brothel), preparing us to notice its variations in each subsequent play. *Pericles'* Greek title, its action, and its final setting in the temple of Diana provide other points of departure. They mark it with an ancient pagan exoticism that will be modified when Shakespeare moves from this play to ancient Britain, the setting for *Cymbeline,* thence to "Bohemia" and "Sicilia" in Christian Europe for *The Winter's Tale,* and thence by way of an island between Milan and Tunis to the epilogue to *The Tempest,* and by it to the great "Globe" itself.

Pericles will be read in several ways: primarily as a story revealing Pericles' delayed individuation and suggesting the value of family relationships in the full maturing of the individual. Not least, it will prove the power of dramatic form to move, through its analogies to ritual, even in the absence of a fully Shakespearean, poetically first-rate, text. I shall argue, finally, that this is an androcentric text: Marina, strong, beautiful, strikingly virtuous, is still characterized (as is her near-namesake, the more passive Mariana in *Measure for Measure*) by her relationships with men. Her strength protects what men most value in her, and her skills in needlework and music are such as to grace their homes.

Date and Text and Sources

Of Shakespeare's four Romances, *Pericles* is certainly the earliest, but little more than that is certain of its date. Either it, or a play by the same name founded on the same old story of Apollonius of Tyre, must have been performed by 1608, since a hack writer, George Wilkins, published that year *The Painfull Adventures of Pericles, Prince of Tyre,* claiming to retell the story of the play of Pericles. The only version of the play printed during Shakespeare's lifetime, a very garbled pirated quarto, was published by Henry Gosson in 1609. A more reputable printer, Edward Blount, had noted his intent to publish both *Pericles* and *Antony and Cleopatra* in the Stationer's Register for May 1608. The date of writing has been estimated to be anywhere from 1606 to 1608. Knowing the haste with which Shakespeare turned out playscripts for his company, we can speculate on a date as late as 1608 for the writing—one I am inclined to favor because of affinities in incident to *Antony and Cleopatra* (also filled with travels through the ancient Mediterranean world) and affinities in style, theme, and incident to the other three Romances, which seem to follow closer upon *Pericles* than by three or four years.

For our purposes, reading and understanding the play as we have it, the actual date of writing is relatively unimportant. But we cannot dismiss as easily other puzzles raised by the one quarto text (1609) that has come down to us anonymously. *Pericles* was not included in the 1623 Folio, which purported to gather all of Shakespeare's plays in one edition. The doubts about his authorship prompted by this fact were supported by other factors. The play is marked by a deep stylistic rift between acts 2 and 3, the first two acts being starker, less richly poetic, than the last three, and quite unlike Shakespeare's usual work. Could *Pericles* have been written by Shakespeare alone? Was it written in collaboration with a writer of lesser talent? Or did Shakespeare himself take up a play of inferior quality and make the extensive changes that render at least the three later acts indisputably his?[1] I think that it is neither necessary nor useful to look for traces of another author in the admittedly weak and scrambled text and in the shift in style between act 2 and act 3. The obscurities and the sheer mistakes in the language of the text are easily explained by the hypothesis that two unskilled reporters garbled what they set down by ear and by memory from stage performances and marked, each with different idiosyncratic faults, the passages they mishandled. But the best reason for dropping speculation about another author lies in the undeniably powerful impact the play makes in production or in an uncritical reading that lets its effects simply happen.[2]

We can be sure that Shakespeare never wrote to satisfy the critical constraints of Ben Jonson or of modern academic readers. If the play is not, at the outset, his, he could have left the bare and awkward simplicity of the first two acts little changed so that he could exploit those characteristics in the acts that do manifest his mature power. If, as I like to think, the play is all his, the same bareness and awkwardness (allowing of course for the many flaws in reporting) can be read as deliberate indicators to lacks in the consciousness of the romantic young prince of Tyre, who ages over many years between acts 3 and 4. From the dangers and adventures in love and loss that mark Pericles' story in acts 1 to 3, we move to other characters, other settings, and the richer story of Marina set forth in imaginative poetry that is unmistakably Shakespeare's. The richness of poetry in act 3 is appropriate to Pericles' development through his brief happiness with Thaisa, and the ending is rendered especially effective by its contrast with the style of the opening acts.

The poetic sparseness at the outset casts all audience attention on the story[3]—originally the ancient romance of Apollonius of Tyre, whose name was changed to Pericles before Shakespeare took the story up. John Gower, whom Shakespeare's version makes the choral presenter and narrator, had told the tale of "Apollonius" in book 8 of his *Confessio Amantis*. As we follow the bare outline of incidents now, we may see resemblances of many sorts to the *Aethiopica,* which may have been about the same age as the earliest versions of this "mouldy" tale.[4]

The Story

Act 1   Gower, as Chorus, explains what the audience is about to see. Pericles, the young prince of Tyre, is to be put to a test in his suit for the hand of the daughter of King Antiochus. He must answer a riddle successfully or forfeit his life. The walls of Antioch are decorated with the decaying heads of earlier suitors.

The "riddle" revealed in the opening scene quite clearly suggests that Antiochus has been incestuously enjoying his daughter. Pericles, reading it thus, flees Antioch in fear. Antiochus sends Thaliard, a servant-courtier, in pursuit with orders to kill Pericles. Back in Tyre, Pericles confers with his trusted senior courtier, Helicanus. They decide that he should flee his country to travel the earth. Thaliard, subsequently arriving and learning this, decides to tell Antiochus that Pericles has "'scap'd the land, to perish at the seas."

Pericles comes by sea to Tharsus. The governor, Cleon, and his wife, Dionyza, are bewailing the famine-stricken state of their city when they hear that his ship is approaching. Expecting he has come to conquer them in their weakness, they marvel to learn that Pericles, in sympathy and goodwill, has brought them corn.

Act 2   A dumb show embedded in Gower's prologue shows Pericles, warned by letter of Thaliard's orders, setting sail again in haste on stormy seas. As the first scene opens, Pericles is shipwrecked on the coast of Pentapolis. Three helpful fishermen tell him that a tournament has been arranged by the good King Simonides for suitors to his daughter's hand. Coincidentally they notice that they have netted a rusty suit of armor. Pericles, recognizing it as his father's, claims it and decides to enter the contest.

Last in the lists to appear before the king and his daughter, Thaisa, Pericles appears the least worthy of all. But he wins the tourney, gaining the favor of both king and daughter: Pericles will marry Thaisa.

Act 3   Again Gower summarizes the events between acts: first the marriage and then the conception of a child. And now Pericles has learned that Antiochus and his daughter have perished and that the men of Tyre will give the crown to Helicanus if their prince does not return. He has set sail from Pentapolis with Thaisa, who is near her time.

A violent storm is tossing the ship when the act opens. Pericles, raging against the unjust sea, hears that his wife has died giving birth to a daughter. To the crew's superstitious insistence that her body be thrown overboard, Pericles gives grudging assent. Sealed in a chest, Thaisa's body washes ashore at Ephesus and is brought to a healer, Cerimon, who uses special potions to revive her. Sailing on unaware, Pericles stops at Tharsus to entrust his newborn daughter, Marina, with her nurse, Lychorida, to Cleon and Dionyza.

Act 4   Many years pass between the acts, Gower tells us, during which Pericles has returned to rule at Tyre, while Marina has grown at Tharsus into a beautiful, virtuous, and accomplished young woman, beside whom Dionyza's daughter pales by comparison. Jealous and ruthless, the queen is plotting Marina's murder.

As the act opens, Marina is gathering flowers for the fresh grave of Lychorida. Commanded by Dionyza to walk with Leonine, the man who is to murder her, Marina learns her danger, pleads innocence of all wrong, and, when Leonine seems adamant, is conveniently seized by pirates, brought to Mytilene, and sold to a bawd, who offers Marina's virginity to the highest bidder.

A dumb show follows in which Pericles, traveling again, is told of his daughter's death. He vows never to cut his hair and to live in perpetual sorrow.

In the brothel, Marina has been preserving her purity by persuasively preaching virtue to her would-be clients. Even Lysimachus, the governor of

Mytilene, responds humbly, if defensively, to her virtue. The bawd, frustrated, tells the despicable Boult that he may deflower Marina by violence to initiate her to the life of vice. But Marina wins over even him, persuading him to spare her so that she can earn her livelihood, and reward her captors, by teaching singing and needlework.

Act 5 When Pericles' ship arrives at Mytilene, Lysimachus meets it. He calls for Marina to minister to Pericles who has been suffering for three months in deep depression. Marina's singing rouses Pericles; he asks her to tell her story and discovers that she is his daughter.

Overcome with joy, Pericles falls asleep and dreams that the goddess Diana is telling him to give thanks at her temple at Ephesus for his good fortune. He arrives there to another scene of restoration. Thaisa, having come there with Cerimon's aid, is now serving as Diana's high priestess. At the end, all virtuous characters are joyously reunited.

Gower's epilogue rounds off the plot. He announces that Cleon and Dionyza have perished, punished by avenging gods for the murder they intended.

Gower and Ritual

The octosyllabic couplets Gower is given to speak are even sparser in style than the flawed blank verse of the early acts. At the outset, before setting the grisly scene at Antioch, he declaims:

> To sing a song that old was sung,
> From ashes ancient Gower is come,
> . . .
> It hath been sung at festivals,
> On ember-eves and holy-ales;
> And lords and ladies in their lives
> Have read it for restoratives:
> The purchase is to make men glorious.

These points we take, if we are alert: it is a very old tale; it has been performed at church and folk festivals; its effects are those of ritual, to restore and glorify the "lords and ladies" and "men" who attend to it. As the first scene opens, Gower points to the heads of unsuccessful suitors that adorn the gates of Antioch before which Pericles is standing. These grisly reminders of mortality, like much in late medieval art, throw us into what Freud calls the realm of "the uncanny," an imaginative space in which we are shaken by the suddenly unfamiliar and threatening aspects of what might normally seem comfortable and familiar—here the scene of courtship.[5]

Just what is so uncanny, as I read it, I leave until I deal with Pericles' quest and transformation, but Freud's essay gives two hints: a severed head is always uncanny, and so also, for the adult male, there is something uncanny about female sexuality, once familiar in the mother but now long strange. Another hint pertains to the effect of this "restorative" fiction: the "apparent death and reanimation of the dead" is a major theme of the uncanny.[6]

In his prologue to act 2, Gower compares Pericles with the "mighty" and incestuous king he is fleeing: Pericles is "a better prince and benign lord / That will prove awful both in deed and word." But clearly he is not awe inspiring yet. The people of Tharsus in gratitude are raising a statue "to make him glorious," but the rest of this prologue shows him fleeing ingloriously once more, a prey to "fortune." The prologue to act 3 repeats the motif of a "sea-tost Pericles." So far neither Gower nor the action has shown us anything but a noble, unfortunate prince who for all his fine intentions (and his evident concern for reputation) does not show the power and control that he has been born to wield.

Gower introduces act 4 with four lines devoted to Pericles and Thaisa and then commands us to bend our minds to Marina. His praise of the now-grown virgin stresses the admiration she earns by her accomplished embroidery, her singing, and her poetry in praise of Diana. He appears again in scene 4: "I do beseech you / To learn of me, who stand i' th' gaps to teach you," he explains, and then places a grieving Pericles before the monument he has had raised at Tharsus to his supposedly dead Marina. The old poet confers pattern and meaning on otherwise disjointed or random events—as when he notes, with apparent approval, Pericles' meek subjection to "Lady Fortune."

The prologue to act 5 characterizes Marina as "like one immortal" and "goddess-like," before returning us to "heavy Pericles." We are to "think this his bark, where[by] what is done in action, more . . . / Shall be discover'd." Gower has used the word "action" before, introducing act 3: "what ensues . . . I nill relate, action may / Conveniently the rest convey." In that instance it clearly refers to stage action, act-ing; but in reference to the plight of passive "heavy Pericles" it takes on a livelier sense. The ritual healing by Marina will transform Pericles: no longer the driven and passive (however piously patient) victim, he will be prepared at last for a life of action fuller than he has yet known.

Gower's epilogue is still sparse, still simple. It reviews the stories of wickedness punished and virtue at last rewarded, and it prays for "new joy" for an audience as patient as the patient Pericles.

In all Gower's stress on patience we are invited to think of Job. Like Pericles, he suffers many losses and trials and—at least in the conventional prose narratives that bracket the poetry of anguished questioning in the book that bears his name—remains an archetype of the "patience" that Helicanus advises for Pericles.[7] In the play Gower plays the role of Job's comforters, choral voices of the old traditional wisdom of reward and punishment. It is a long way to Shakespeare's Romances from the Bible and the miracle plays that were still being staged in rural England at the time of Shakespeare's early comedies.[8] Yet Pericles, as Job and Everyman, and Gower, as moral-drawing commentator, have reminded many of the old religious drama. For that reason, I found the playing of Gower in a recent production by a flamboyantly dressed black gospel singer startlingly appropriate.[9] Like a miracle play, gospel song serves to convey an old story of death, resurrection, and transforming salvation to a simple audience. Gospel music, like a miracle play and like *Pericles,* both celebrates and makes mythic sense of events that would otherwise seem random, disjointed, chaotic.

When this chapter is complete, my differences with Gower as interpreter will be clearer. For now, let it suffice that I see him standing for an old religion, serving a highly practical function in the economy of a complex story, and signaling the power of ritual to transform. By reducing the episodic patterns of the story to ritualistic outlines, Gower highlights the structural repetitions within the story. We see the parallels between Antiochus and his daughter and Cleon and Dionyza drawn in the epilogue; we hear the storm-tossed seas threatening Pericles again and again and start to see them as a metaphor for life; we recognize the parallels between Thaisa and Marina in Pericles' life and consciousness. And then, although certainly ancient Gower does not put it to us this way, the structural imagination he has aroused in us draws further parallels concerning fathers, daughters, wives, and sons, and we come to find the structures uncanny and ultimately very revealing. This play, as Charles Nicholl has suggested, takes on the power of alchemy.[10] By showing us to ourselves, it offers a temporary change that, assimilated, has power to change us more permanently.

Characters as Types

Most of the figures to which I now turn are not richly characterized: they are cardboard-thin personae, masks, types, and as such they are characteristic of any other romance. The very diction of the play emphasizes the typology:

"Ancient Gower"; "great Antiochus" (whose given name signals to the bibli-
cally literate that his might serves evil); Helicanus, "Fit counsellor and servant for a prince"; "the good king Simonides"; Thaisa, "Beauty's child,
whom Nature gat / For men to see, and seeing wonder at." The list could be
extended; virtually all of the characters, despite the occasional moments of
individuality they may enjoy, are typecast. Even Pericles and Marina, certainly the fullest characters, remain with us, long after their features fade, as
types of patience and purity.

For convenience, I shall discuss the lesser characters in typological catego-
ries, although most conform to more than one category. In the first scene, we
see the confrontation between two rulers, one a generation older than the
other, one bad and one good, one tyrannical and the other fearfully
nonassertive. The play opens, then, on the category of rulers. Later, in addition to Pericles and Antiochus, it will show us Cleon, Simonides, Lysimachus,
the regent Helicanus—and various women who, for bad or good, come to
rule the rulers.

Rulers and the Theme of Rule

The theme of rule pervades all of Shakespeare's plays. He was writing
under a monarchy, in a period when hierarchies were envisioned at all levels of
human and superhuman experience. Let us imagine, briefly, how his audiences tended to see their world—or rather their interlocking worlds.

In the visible heavens, the sun is king, but above, invisibly, ranks of angels
extend to the highest invisible heaven where God is ruler of all. On earth,
similarly, all is ordered in ranks. Just as each nation has its ruler under God,
with his courtiers under him, landowning and mercantile classes below them,
and artisans, laborers, slaves in custom-controlled ranks still further down, so
also animals, birds, plants, minerals, and all other created things are ordered
in ranks. So far, our imaginings are too simple. Human individuals reflect in
psychological microcosm the heaven of spirit, the social organism in their
mid-souls, and the earth in their bodies. They are cross-connected to their
counterparts in other orders, as well as to fellow members of the same order.
Similarly the lion, king of the beasts, has affinities of beasthood with the land
beasts below him and affinities of another sort with the rulers of the nations,
with the sun, with the eagle, king of the birds, with all golden flowers that
turn their heads to the sun, and with gold, the highest of minerals. The examples could be multiplied endlessly—and were in ancient treatises on these
matters.[11] Shakespeare and his Renaissance contemporaries, though they

often questioned and adapted these ancient patterns, never lost the conviction that order was desirable and good.

When we think in these terms of rulers, serious issues arise. When the ruler is good, he sustains a good order. When the ruler is bad or unwise, what about hierarchy as a principle? Can, or should, one of lower rank oppose a legitimate, but evil, ruler? Shakespeare, with apparent impartiality, had explored this issue in the history plays. In Antiochus he raises it again, marking this play at the outset as a consideration of order and power in kingdoms, as well as in the lesser "kingdoms" of the family and of the inner self in which it involves itself even more.

The very name of the king of Antioch would strike caution into the heart of a Renaissance audience. Antiochus was the name of a series of oppressive rulers over the Jews in the apocryphal book of Maccabees. They were self-styled as mighty; one titled himself "Epiphanes" to claim that he showed forth the divine. But when Pericles (who, within this pagan fiction has no reason to know the Bible) approaches his Antiochus at the grisly, head-decorated gates and sees the king's beautiful daughter approaching, he acknowledges the might of the older ruler with neither caution nor irony. He implores the gods to make him "son to great Antiochus" and associates this hoped-for father with "all good men" as he "bequeath[s] a happy peace" to him should he, Pericles, fail in his dangerous suit. To the daughter, whom he sees for the first time, he declares an "unspotted fire of love": he is "ready for the way of life or death" (1.1.54–55). When, later in Tyre, Helicanus tells Pericles "to bear with patience / Such griefs as you do lay upon yourself" (1.2.65–66), he confirms the audience's reactions to the young romantic's rashness. When Pericles interprets the transparent riddle, his response is as immediate and firm as his decision to seek the dangerous princess was rash. As his love has been "unspotted," it will now have nothing to do with damaged property: "For he's no man on whom perfections wait / That, knowing sin within, will touch the gate. . . . Good sooth, I care not for you."

For Pericles, the central character in this story is himself—a young ruler who, like Hamlet before him, thinks rulers must be perfect men with perfect consorts. We may sense that this damsel who has already shown an inclination toward him (1.1.60–61) may be, like Ophelia, in some father-ridden distress. But it never occurs to Pericles to risk cleansing Antioch by killing an evil father and rescuing the lady; he has come bravely seeking a bride unparalleled, and now that he knows this lady to be sullied, that is the end of it. The reasons for his responses will be sought later; meanwhile, we see his flight from Antiochus as belated caution, a junior ruler's refusal to risk, as Hamlet eventually risks, a challenge to the father figure, evil as he clearly is.

We do not see Antiochus after the first act: he has fulfilled his functions. His evil contrasts with the goodness of the young hero and provides the impetus (in his command that Thaliard kill Pericles) that keeps this episodic story going for the next two acts.

The next ruler on stage with Pericles is Cleon. Whereas Antiochus has threatened Pericles, Cleon feels threatened by Pericles before he learns of the aid the stranger brings. Before Pericles lands, Cleon, passive but eloquent in misery, reminds us of Richard II proposing, under threat, to sit down and "tell sad stories of the deaths of kings."[12] He invites Dionyza to "rest us here / And by relating tales of others' griefs / See if 'twill teach us to forget our own." She, more practical, sees that "that were to blow at fire in hope to quench it," yet in the role of dutiful wife, she listens and provides choric response whenever Cleon takes breath in his litany of sorrow.

After Pericles has arrived and announced his gift, he brushes aside the prayerful response of "all" at Tharsus: "We do not look for reverence, but for love / And harbourage." The initial impression that Pericles is the stronger of these two rulers reverses itself when he meekly seeks sanctuary in Cleon's city. His final speech in this act confirms the reversal in notes of fatalistic passivity: "welcome we'll accept; feast here awhile / Until our stars that frown lend us a smile."

Alike in the uneasy equilibrium of fearful apprehension, host and guest differ in another respect: Cleon distrusts the world and any stranger until events prove him wrong; Pericles is predisposed to trust, trusting even Antiochus until he has read the riddle. After we hear, in Gower's third prologue, of Cleon's passivity in the face of Dionyza's treachery against Marina, we see both lowered by their passivity: Cleon in moral stature, and Pericles, retrospectively, for lack of judgment in entrusting his child to virtual strangers. Dionyza at this point has become a female counterpart to Antiochus in the strength of her villainy. Pericles remains helpless, years after the initial encounter, in the face of this evil.

But earlier, in act 2, we have met a strong and positive image of rule at Pentapolis in the good king Simonides. Like Antiochus, and like Richard II, this king delights in the ceremony of kingship. His tournament, arranged to settle the hand of Thaisa in that of the victor, is a ritual celebration of his power over both his daughter and her suitors. But unlike Richard at the trial by combat between Mowbray and Bolingbroke, Simonides retains full control over the proceedings, and unlike Antiochus, he honestly does intend to wed his daughter to the worthiest contestant. His wisdom is signaled early to the audience in his responses when the courtiers scoff at Pericles' rusty armor:

"Opinion's but a fool that makes us scan / [by] The outward habit . . . the inward man."[13]

Pericles' responses to "the good" Simonides at the victory banquet bear comparison with his interaction with Antiochus. Before reading the riddle, he openly told Antiochus that he aspired to be his son by marriage; now, facing Simonides, he muses in a similar response, but deeper and more personal, and finds the king "like to [his] father's picture" in his glory. Pericles' eyes are on the great ruler, to whose status, wearing his own father's armor, he aspires through marriage. Thaisa, just lines before, has been more direct in yearning for Pericles, although her words are spoken aside: "All viands that I eat do seem unsavoury / Wishing him my meat." Not until the fifth scene, when (once bitten) the suitor-prince is taking care to ensure that Simonides does not oppose the match, does Pericles turn his words directly to Thaisa, and then first to enlist her aid against her "angry father." Only when Simonides gives up his pretense of opposition does Pericles speak forthrightly to Thaisa of his love—he loves her "as my life the blood that fosters it." But even in this he has had to be prompted by Thaisa. Her daughterly spunk in both scenes accents his timidity.

Lysimachus, governor of Mytilene, is the last male ruler we meet in *Pericles*. His appearance as would-be client to Marina at the brothel seriously compromises his majesty, as she is quick to point out to him (4.6.78–80). When this ruler falls under the sway of her moral rhetoric and abandons his apparent intention to enjoy her virginal body, he, like Cleon, is ruled by a woman. But unlike Cleon, Lysimachus is ruled by a woman's virtue, not vice, to his own eventual, and Marina's immediate, advantage.

When Gower's epilogue finds Cleon and Dionyza justly punished by the gods for "murder . . . not done, but meant" we need not quarrel with the judgment, but it give us reason to ponder Lysimachus's questionable presence in the brothel. In his Sermon on the Mount, Jesus says that to look on a woman with lust is to commit adultery with her in the heart (Matt. 5:28). Why does nothing in the text hold Lysimachus ultimately guilty of conduct unbecoming to a ruler? Just what did he "mean" in coming to the brothel? His protestation to Marina that he came "with no ill intent" is supported by no alternative explanation for his presence. Although his leave-taking—"If thou dost / Hear from me, it shall be for thy good" (4.6.115–16)—can be read in retrospect as a hint at a later marriage, it is improbable that Lysimachus came looking for a bride in this unlikely place. A ruler needs a bride by birth worthy of his hand and by experience unsullied. The moral inconsistencies in Lysimachus can be countered by the argument that characters in romance are not to be questioned seriously, since, like the chess pieces

Ferdinand and Miranda resemble in Prospero's game, they are always subordinated to the pattern of their disposition on the board. Shakespeare does seem to have felt the actions of Lysimachus to be problematic: none of his counterparts in earlier versions is made to protest innocence of intent. His lack of motivation remains a fault, a gap, in the whole—but not a serious gap, since Shakespeare's prime concern in the restoration of Pericles is with the perfection of Marina, not of her suitor. Even if their brides are not, male rulers are permitted their shares in human frailty.

Courtiers: The Morality of Obedience

The political issues raised in the story by the sins and lesser faults of rulers can be demonstrated through Helicanus of Tyre and Thaliard of Antioch. We meet Helicanus on Pericles' return from Antioch, first preaching the evils of flattery to his fellow courtiers and then taking part with his prince in a perfunctory ritual of power and subservience (1.2.51–65).

Helicanus speaks out forthrightly only after his declaration of submission and then only on the invitation, "What would'st thou have me do?" But his sententious advice, "To bear with patience / Such griefs as you do lay upon yourself," translates to a strong rebuke. He is telling Pericles to take his medicine like a man; he has asked for it. Helicanus more than gets away with this boldness. His prince recognizes the wisdom he himself still lacks and thanks the "physician" who "ministers a potion unto me." In so doing, Pericles shows his own fair-mindedness, and, from another perspective, the hollowness of his earlier charade of awesome retributive power. In the good state of Tyre, it is clear, an honest courtier may, on proper occasion, dare to offer critical advice to his ruler.

Thaliard, in contrast, shows a fear of the mighty Antiochus fully justified by the heads decorating that king's palace walls. When Thaliard arrives in Tyre, he muses, "Here I must kill King Pericles; and if I do it not, I am sure to be hang'd at home: 'tis dangerous." Then, uncomfortable in this admission of timidity, he justifies himself by a legalism: "if a king bid a man be a villain, he's bound by the indenture of his oath to be one" (1.3.7–8). That Thaliard has no taste for his assignment is clear when he learns that Pericles has fled Tyre. Rather than follow, Thaliard proposes to tell Antiochus that the younger ruler has "'scap'd the land, to perish at the seas." The lie, more than the self-justification by oath that cut in a different direction, is justified by circumstance, but Thaliard has been unavoidably contaminated by the evil at Antioch. In the larger structure, both he and Antioch stand judged by the counterexamples of Helicanus and Tyre.

We find these issues reinforced later in the play when Leonine, commanded upon oath by Dionyza to kill Marina, seizes her as if to obey before the conveniently attacking pirates force him to abandon her to a different evil. When he waits to make sure the new captors carry her off, because "if she remain, / Whom they have ravish'd must by me be slain" (4.1.101–2), Leonine's motivation is confirmed as self-preservation (although a patriarchal audience might welcome for Marina such a release from the shame worse than death).

Obedience to the wrongful commands of a ruler had of course been questioned long before Shakespeare's time. Plato's Seventh Letter records his own flight from Sicily to avoid compliance with the rule of the tyrant Dionysius, and his *Defence* and *Phaedo* show Socrates choosing death over compliance with the edicts of an oligarchic regime whose ends he has repudiated.[14] Such questioning of absolute authority had gained new prominence in Renaissance England: Sir Thomas More's sturdy independence under a ruler he judged wrong must have been strong in the memory of Shakespeare's audiences. So, too, would they remember characters in his earlier plays who, to their own danger, drew clear distinctions between public fealty and private virtue. "My life thou shalt command, but not my shame," Sir Thomas Mowbray told Richard II; "Be Kent unmannerly, / When Lear is mad," Lear's courtier-"physician" told his king, applying to himself the age-old metaphor of healing that Pericles applies gratefully to Helicanus. Moral integrity in such figures as Socrates and Jesus had long been seen as healing; the stock figure of the Doctor in miracle plays had always carried (by oblique reference to "the good physician," Jesus) moral as well as physical significance. The good courtier, sacrificially, can heal the state.

On the linked issue of the taking of oaths, Jesus had stressed the value of a simple integrity like Helicanus' when he commanded, "Swear not at all . . . But let your communication be Yea, yea; Nay, nay: for whatsoever is more than these cometh of evil" (Matt. 5:34, 37). Pagan though this fiction is, Pericles follows the New Testament ethic when he brushes aside Cleon's oaths of promise: "I believe you . . . Without your vows." Later Pericles will not ask Marina to swear to the fantastic story she tells, nor, after the dream of Diana, will he give oath to come to Ephesus. His word will be a simple yea: "I will obey thee." In the final scene, the fact that no oaths are interchanged between Pericles and Lysimachus reinforces in each ruler the image of integrity restored. That Helicanus's integrity requires no reinforcement by oath is a telling proof of his virtue.

Helicanus, then, functions primarily in the play as a model courtier-servant, much like Pisanio in *Cymbeline,* Camillo in *The Winter's Tale,* and

Gonzalo in *The Tempest*. One subsidiary function relates to this courtier's advanced age. The play needs a parental figure to underscore Pericles' youth and psychological immaturity. When our interpreting eye is looking at familial and generational matters more than at affairs of state, Helicanus becomes a good father figure, anticipating Simonides and balancing the evil of Antiochus. No inconsistency is involved in such parallel readings. Since, according to Renaissance philosophy, parallels among the body politic, the family, and the inner psyche were common, it made sense in the economy of the fiction to assign superimposed roles to a single figure.

When, in act 1, we see Helicanus as a benign father, humoring and guiding a promising but rash young man, we learn something about Pericles' psychological underdevelopment at the outset. When we see the same Helicanus in mid-play patiently refusing to rule Tyre indefinitely, calling Pericles home from Pentapolis after his marriage to take up his responsibilities, and much later see him in the final act still caring for the king, now immobilized by despair, the impression hardens that Pericles suffers seriously from some mode of arrested development. He matches the archetypal figure the Jungians call the *puer aeternus*. The phrase evokes words spoken in *The Winter's Tale* by Polixenes, friend and childhood "twin" to Leontes, describing their younger selves: "Two lads that thought there was no more behind / But such a day tomorrow as today, / And to be boy eternal." I'll have more to say of the *puer* archetype later, but for now we turn to another group of characters, the women.

The "Women" of the Play: Queens, Nurse, Healer, Bawd, Goddess

To interpret the "bad" women and the "good" women in *Pericles,* to ponder what is "bad" and "good" about them, opens our perception to patterns latent in human relationships that Shakespeare wove into his mimesis of experience but would not, probably, in a more hierarchical age, have interpreted as we now are inclined to do.

Dionyza, clearly a demonic type, is the one ruling "queen" in *Pericles,* since Thaisa never sees Tyre during the dramatic action. In her barely motivated wickedness, I have already compared Dionyza to the tyrannical Antiochus. Both misuse their power in response to personal lusts—his of a directly sexual nature and hers a lust for power and position for the daughter she sees threatened by Marina's virtues. If Dionyza's motivation seems slightly less egocentric than that of Antiochus, because it is centered on her daughter (a displaced image of her own sexuality), her actions are even more reprehensible from a conventional perspective. Her ritualistic compliance to Cleon when we first meet them shows that she knows she is not a lawful ruler. She works her evil furtively against the better, but weaker, moral judgment of her husband. Like Cymbeline's queen, she would represent to Shakespeare's audiences what John Knox dubbed (in the title of his polemic against Mary Queen of Scots) "the monstrous regiment of women."[15] Women were not, typically, regarded as born to rule but to be ruled, not to exert hurtful power and strike fear into men but to nurture and heal. Elizabeth, who had ruled successfully in the very recent past, had been careful to refer to herself as a "prince" when her legitimate power was at issue, and, by cultivating her virginal image as "mother" to the nation, to associate herself with the peerless Queen of Heaven as a nurturing, saving, quasi-magical figure. She thus had escaped the taint of active sexuality that can lead a Dionyza, like a beast, to pervert the essence of motherhood in aggressively seeking advantage for her young.

Dionyza's villainy is clearly perverse by the standards of the world Shakespeare inhabited. For a woman to "rule" at all, except ceremonially as consort to a king, is highly dangerous. The "power" a woman can and should exert is not power but service: nurturing and healing, knitting up, not rending, the fabric of society and of the lives of others.

Although Thaisa is daughter to a king and wife to a ruler, Pericles, she does not fit the type of a ruling queen. Her life as queen lies beyond the boundaries of the story. Further, for the consort to a ruler to rule even ceremonially, her husband must, in some sense, be in command. Although Pericles presumably does rule during the missing years covered by Gower's prologue to act 4, we see him thereafter only on storm-tossed seas or helplessly in thrall to grief. Thaisa is thus distanced even from ceremonial ruling by her husband's character, which is not prepared to take full command until the very end of the play.[16]

Thaisa, a queen in name only, functions primarily in the familial patterns of *Pericles*. As the archetypal good wife and mother, she offers a foil to Dionyza but, through no fault of her own and through most of the action, remains almost as absent as the mother of Pericles who never figures in name or reminiscence. In Pericles-Everyman's quest through life, he lacks a nurturing wife and mother figure except for the brief period of nuptial happiness before he loses Thaisa, whose own motherhood is suspended from the time she loses consciousness in childbirth until her reunion with the grown Marina. The touching exchange between mother and daughter at Ephesus—"My heart / Leaps to be gone into my mother's bosom" and "Bless'd, and mine own"—

reinforces the images (especially in "bosom") of Thaisa as good wife and mother and (especially in "Bless'd") of Marina as the archetype of Virgin. Lychorida, brief though her appearances are in the play, is the archetypal nurse, mother substitute, protector of the young. Her death, reported in the prologue to act 3, leaves Marina vulnerable to Dionyza. That the role of nurturing protector must be played by a mother substitute, not a true parent, one who does not live as long as she is needed, fits the literary conventions of romance wherein highborn children are often separated from their parents to endure danger. It also fits the social conventions of the ruling classes in Renaissance England.[17] But it suggests that Shakespeare sees something off-kilter when affairs of state and society take precedence over the direct nurturing of children—that is, when the masculine activities of power and rule take precedence over the more feminine works of love.[18] In the storm scene at sea when she brings news of Thaisa's "death" to Pericles, Lychorida plays another role. She takes on attributes of both Gower and Helicanus when she counsels, "Be manly, and take comfort . . . Patience, good sir / Even for this charge." Here she is the traditional voice telling the suffering "Job" and king what his deportment must be in this time of testing, and, as strong adviser, reinforcing in him, ironically, the emotional passivity that is so at odds with "manly" actions. We remember Macduff, also counseled to take comfort and "dispute it like a man" when he learns that Macbeth, with his Lady in perverse masculinity, has taken from him "all [his] pretty ones." When Macduff responds "I shall do so; / But I must also feel it as a man," he redefines the "manliness" he lacked in his earlier flight from Scotland so that it now includes the emotions contingent on love.[19] Pericles responds to Lychorida's advice with an almost-feminine sweetness toward the babe in his arms, perfectly appropriate to the circumstances, but it will be some years yet before he can stop oscillating between the "manly" and the patiently passive in his own psyche. Lychorida's failure to "heal" him, to make him hale and whole, is typical of the societies he speaks for, those who define "manliness" in one-sided terms.

I come now to the healer, Cerimon, a man whose function in reviving Thaisa parallels that of Marina toward Pericles and contrasts with that of the wicked stepmother-queen in *Cymbeline.* My decision to discuss him with the women of the play has to do with the typology of healing, of making whole, and nothing to do with an unmanly "character"; Cerimon, as befits "a lord of Ephesus," his description in the *dramatis personae,* is decisive and effective.

We learn, before the casket enclosing Thaisa's "corse" is brought in, that Cerimon is a man of charity who holds his "virtue and cunning"—his power and skill in medicine—higher than the wealth he also enjoys. When he predicts the death of the "poor man" just brought to him (3.2.7–8), we are alerted to his skill in "physick" but warned not to take him simply as a miracle worker. He works with nature and natural substances to effect his cures. Like the magician-physician Paracelsus,[20] he knows the "blest infusions / That dwell in vegetives, in metals, stones" and the transformative cures for "the disturbances that / Nature works" (3.2.25–38). His name (found also in Gower) suggests ceremony[21] and, in conjunction with his work in physical substances, suggests sacraments of sacrifice and lustration, both pagan and Christian. Sacramental rites channel divine power through natural substances to work transformation.

The authority that Cerimon commands before the casket is opened turns his words—"They were too rough / That threw her in the sea"—into an emphatic rebuke: Pericles has yielded too easily to the sailors' superstitions. His further words are ambiguous. We might take his restoration of Thaisa as the miraculous event suggested by "Death may usurp on nature many hours / And yet the fire of life kindle again / The o'erpress'd spirits"; yet a few lines later, he says, "She hath not been entranc'd above five hours" (3.2.84–85, 96), suggesting coma, not death. Shakespeare needs it both ways: romance thrives on awe-inspiring marvels and miracles, but the "meaning" of romance requires that we relate the marvels to a life that can parallel our own. If we, participating in this mimesis, are to learn from it, Pericles' abandonment of the stricken Thaisa must be, more than a burial at sea, a passive sin of omission against a living woman. It may not, I suggest later, be the only such sin.

Cerimon's further function is linked to the temple of the virgin goddess, Diana of Ephesus, whose name Thaisa has invoked on awakening. Her vow to take "a vestal livery" since "My wedded lord, I ne'er shall see again"—too hasty as that may seem to an audience that has already seen much scurrying around the Mediterranean world—is accepted without question by Cerimon. He obviously values such service, promising to take her to the temple and offering to have his niece attend her. He is present with Thaisa at the temple when, many years later, Pericles arrives for their reunion. Ceremony clearly has much to do with the great restorative changes of life.

The last character to figure in this grouping is a woman never dignified by proper name as certain of her ancient profession have been in earlier plays—the "Bawd," in Shakespeare's term. She draws none of the sympathy we give to Mistress Quickly in her obvious affection for Falstaff, and to Mistress Overdone in the distress she feels for Claudio and the charity she extends to the innocent offspring of her whores. The bawd, this latter whoremonger, has no heart of gold. She jokes unfeelingly about disease and death and sees Marina as a mere commodity, disturbing in her refusal to learn her trade. A total negation of life-supporting, nurturing womanhood, the bawd stands with Dionyza on the negative side of the ledger against the positive Lychorida and the even more positive Thaisa and Marina. That her ugly henchman, Boult, shows more decency eventually than she, reinforces the utter blackness of her image and justifies his bearing of a name.

The other "wicked" and unnamed woman of the play, the daughter of Antiochus, is an ambiguous cipher in the nightmarish opening scene, to which I now turn.

Pericles and Marina: The *Puer* and the Virgin

> I am no viper, yet I feed
> On mother's flesh, which did me breed.
> I sought a husband, in which labour
> I found that kindness in a father.
> He's father, son, and husband mild;
> I mother, wife, and yet his child:
> How they may be, and yet in two,
> As you will live, resolve it you.
>   (1.1.65–72)

Perverse as it may seem to begin an extended discussion of a "good" father and daughter with this passage, I am following the lead of the text, which, offering the riddle in the first scene, establishes its centrality to the story. The ostensible subjects of the riddle appear only in the first scene. Thereafter Antiochus is an absent paternal bogeyman, fear of whom bedevils Pericles, and his corrupted daughter disappears to be replaced by a diametrically opposed figure, the pure Thaisa. The primacy of this particular incestuous pair does not give the riddle its pride of place, but the tangle of relationships between the sexes and generations that it points to—the central themes of the play. Although Pericles is a ruler, and the rule of outer kingdoms assumes subsidiary importance in the plot, it is the journey toward self-rule in the male soul that *Pericles* at length demonstrates. Only when the complexities in family and sexual relationships are ordered by understanding and by healthy interpersonal love can those who wield outward power learn to rule themselves. And only those who rule themselves well—in this as in all the other Romances—deserve their control over events in the body politic.

The riddle serves an important structural purpose as well. Unlike *The Winter's Tale,* whose two halves form a tragicomic diptych, this episodic Romance declares itself one play through the complex patterns of the riddle.

Pericles' trials, Marina's trials, and the saving interrelationship that develops between father and daughter are comprehended in the morally neutral couplet at the heart of the otherwise suspect riddle: "He's father, son, and husband mild; / I mother, wife, and yet his child." Every man, and every woman, has three potential roles to play in life—child, spouse, and parent—and begins to learn them in the parental home. The roles correlate, oversimplified of course, to passivity, cooperation, and authority, respectively, any one of which may be found appropriate in a given situation. The mature soul has all three in her repertory (the soul, psyche, anima, is female symbolically as well as linguistically) and has the wisdom to respond in the right role at a given time.

When Pericles responds with immediate comprehension to the riddle that, ostensibly at least in Gower's narrative, has stumped all previous suitors, the situation invites a variety of responses. We wonder how the other suitors could have missed the implications of incest. Does Pericles somehow bring to the reading something that helps him interpret it (as we do also, finding it equally readable)? Is he less innocent of incestuous feeling than his hapless predecessors? He must share something of the experiences that lead us, as participating onlookers, to read it easily.

I have already offered clues to Pericles' psychic predicament as a young Everyman; it is time now to develop them more fully. In preparation, let us consider the descriptions depth psychology offers of the *puer aeternus,* eternal boy, the archetype of the youthful idealistic hero of romance. Most of us meet this archetype in our inner kingdoms as we grow up. Women as well as men know "him" and can be in his power when their active, assertive, "masculine" traits are directed toward high spiritual goals. The *puer,* often a force for good along life's way, needs eventually to be put and kept in his place as one of many cooperating archetypes in a richly constellating psyche.

The *puer aeternus,* as Marie-Louise von Franz outlines his history, goes back to Iacchus, the child-god of the Eleusinian mysteries in Ovid's *Metamorphoses.* Like most other male consorts of great mother goddesses, he is identified with life, death, and resurrection. As the man who "remains too long in adolescent psychology," the *puer* seeks a mother goddess, "a perfect woman" who will "satisfy his every need." Each time he projects his hopes on a woman he faces the disappointment of finding her "an ordinary human being."[22] In life this process may produce a Don Juan or a misogynist. In romantic fiction, a genre made for *puer* heroes, it produces, to say the least, episodic plots like that of *Pericles.*

When Pericles solves the riddle easily, it may be that, from his depths, he recognizes the yearning for the love of mother, wife, and child in one woman that the world repudiates (if it is acted out) as incestuous. Lacking the post-Freudian sophistication that absolves men through the universality of such fantasies, Pericles is struck by the horror that Freud describes as "uncanny." The familiar (Pericles' own quest for love in a sexual "place"; his desire to make Antiochus his father) is now distanced in the unfamiliar vision of severed heads ranged on the barrier walls, marking the "father" as enemy, oedipally monstrous in his sexuality. Seeing himself as spiritually above such defilement, Pericles separates himself totally from this dangerous place.

The *puer*-heroes of romance often rescue pure maidens from dragons, completing their quest for self-knowledge. But the "dragon" of evil here, remotely given shape in "she an eater of her mother's flesh" and "both like serpents," is no object for Pericles' heroism; the king's daughter, "child" of "foul incest," is no maiden. I have already noted that the unnamed lady seems ready for a change, favoring Pericles to win. But because she is a cardboard character—no Ophelia in pathos—we drop her here. The point is all but made.

The story, openly, is of a monstrous evil and danger, but when we interpret the improbabilities of this romance for their mythic suggestiveness we come to wonder how much of the uncanny horror of the scene is being projected from the *puer*'s still unbalanced psyche.

When Pericles is again tossed into the chaos of shifting emotional roles, he has enjoyed brief happiness in Pentapolis with Thaisa, only to lose her when each must move into the role of parent. The conventions of romance provide the storm and the trance, but psychology suggests that this *puer*'s readiness to abandon the all-too-mortal body of his goddess-spouse might be stemming from his own confusions at a crucial point in life. After all, he has chartered the ship and should be in command. That he believes Thaisa dead too easily (Cerimon is a trustworthy judge) may stem from his unarticulated realization that never more will this perfect mother-woman devote herself entirely to him. The great danger for the *puer*, says von Franz in a pertinent image, is that he neurotically tends to put his "problem . . . in a box and shut the lid on it."[23] Fortunately for Thaisa, Pericles did see that the lid was "close . . . caulked and bitumed."

Transferring his affections at Lychorida's urging to the infant Marina, Pericles soon separates himself from her as well. Within the fiction the action makes sense—"the babe / Cannot hold out to Tyrus." But that he waits until she is grown to "fetch his daughter home" opens a gap that even Gower does not fill. Pericles seems simply to be returning to the pattern of the *puer* who, unengaged, is always on the move, everlastingly "switching," but he seems also to be waiting until time has prepared his daughter to fill a nurturing role.

He waits so long that he falls prey to the saturnine depression that plagues the *senex,* the *puer*'s polar complement. Marina's healing power goes to work not on a "boy eternal" but on a man prematurely aged by the beard he has grown in grief over the "death" of the daughter he has neglected to seek for her whole life's span.[24]

What the *puer* keeps seeking, of course, is his mother in the person of the virgin-goddess. For Pericles, Thaisa has filled the role well until her real motherhood, when the frailty that simulated death marked her as mere mortal, and the unmistakable evidence of her physical sexuality marked her as "uncanny." We see her regain the virginal image at length when, separated from her "lord," she devotes herself to the life of a vestal of Diana.

The Virgin archetype, which fits both Thaisa and Marina in their separate ways, has too complex a structure and history to describe here fully.[25] But certain attributes of the Virgin Mary, arising from the masculine ways of thinking during the Christian era, and of other "virgins" encountered in the myths of other cultures, will illuminate this fiction. Mary has the perfection that the idealistic *puer* seeks—and that perfection depends upon, and shapes, the miracles that distance her from the fleshly sexuality that taints every other daughter of Eve. Not only do biblical and apocryphal narratives declare the "virgin birth" of Jesus, they insist that Mary, his mother, remained a virgin throughout her life and that she herself was immaculately conceived and miraculously "assumed" into heaven. With a perfection like this in mind, the *puer* who insists on something better than Antiochus's daughter will have problems after he has enjoyed, even lawfully, a "perfect" virgin bride. Childbirth always exposes the earthiness of woman—unless it is attended by angelic choirs and a star, not by the storm at sea that signifies chaotic, dragonish, matter.

The virgin, as complex archetype, has attributes not typical of the Virgin Mary. In ancient tales, like that of the aged King David (in 1 Kings 1), a "young virgin" may be sought for the magical power of healing the older male projects on her youthful beauty and vitality. Marina's ministrations to her speechless and bearded father are more effective—and less obviously sexual—than those of Abishag the Shunamite to King David, but the archetypal impetus is the same. Kings, not much use if they are "stricken in years" and passive, need the potent magic ancient wisdom, heeded by Lysimachus, hopes for from a virgin.[26] Similarly, younger, more active kings in ancient story seek the perfection and power of a virgin in their consorts, that the power may be transmitted magically through their unions to the benefit of the kings' lands. The same attributes that lead Lysimachus, like a good host, to bring Marina to the stricken Pericles lead him to seek her magic for himself in marriage, as he once sought it less honorably in the brothel.

In pagan lore "virginity" need not entail sexual innocence (as in Marina) or "widowed" abstinence (as in Thaisa at the temple). The virgin, whether a goddess like Diana or a vestal acolyte, was fully independent of masculine control. She stands thus as a symbol of the autonomous soul, of the individuated anima. Marina's power to protect herself in the brothel participates both in the quasi-magic of sexual innocence and in the psychological strength of one who can rely on her own decisive independence.[27]

Within the fiction, the reunion of Marina and Pericles heals the father because his months of silent withdrawal have been initiated by the news of her "death" in Tharsus. It restores what has been lost (a theme of romance the next three plays will also develop) and knits itself into the fully happy ending that requires the further restoration of Thaisa. But if we ask why, for Pericles, the restoration of spouse must wait upon the restoration of daughter, we evoke interesting insights. The first clue takes us into the dream world of the protagonist, as his story takes us into our own. He cannot be united with the wife he believes he has lost to death until Diana intervenes in vision, commanding him to come to Ephesus. But what has taken Diana so long to appear to him? The query leads us to the prolonged interchange with Marina that precedes the vision. When Marina has identified herself to her anonymous father as Marina, "daughter to King Pericles," the story line has seemed complete—but Pericles is not easily satisfied. He asks her to "tell me now / My drown'd queen's name, as in the rest you said / Thou hast been godlike perfect." Marina names Thaisa, twice for emphasis, before Pericles calls for blessings on her, requests fresh garments to signify his changed state,[28] and opens conversation with Helicanus and Lysimachus in tones of equal strength.

The naming of Thaisa is the key. In her name, Pericles acknowledges her individuality. Now not just the "virgin"-spouse, she becomes a particular beloved woman. By asking for, and responding to, Thaisa's name, Pericles leaves behind the "dead queen" who was no more than consort and adjunct to his own perfections. He now acknowledges her independence as a person—her deeper "virginity." Only at this point is it appropriate for Diana, an autonomous goddess who does not take her attributes or power from a male god, to intervene.

Thaisa does not lack independence at her father's court. She defers to Simonides less often than Pericles. But marriage and pregnancy drop her into the dependence that requires her to attend Diana for safety and stature. Had Thaisa been restored to Pericles before Marina, he might not have found her gentle presence enough to prompt his own transition to full autonomy. But the strength Marina has found in her suffering can shock him into recognizing that it puts his to girlish shame (5.1.134–37).

Ironically, the final act that confirms Pericles in the autonomy he was born to assume prepares Marina to abandon hers as a virgin. Lysimachus does not woo his bride. He hints condescendingly at the brothel that she may hear from him but waits until he knows her royal birth to propose the match to her father, who then decides and announces his decision. Marina is reduced to auditor and puppet.

In the denouement, Marina and Thaisa are promised a share of rule, but by male fiat and under male control. Pericles announces that he will rule with Thaisa in her home state of Pentapolis and turn Tyre over to Lysimachus and Marina. That the succession in each instance is through the female lends support to all arguments that women, and the feminine principles by which they live, are more important in these Romances than in other Shakespearean genres. But the irony remains. *Pericles* is a play about a man and by a man, forgiving flawed male characters for their human failings but presenting its women as perfect or perfectly wicked. It is a man's romance, serving a man's dream.

Not until the next Romance does Shakespeare give us a woman as important to the drama as any man. It may be no coincidence that one strand of *Cymbeline*'s plot leads Imogen through a prolonged nightmare.

Chapter Three

"Great Jupiter . . . Appear'd to me": *Cymbeline*

For its spatial setting, *Cymbeline* returns home to Shakespeare's Britain. But temporally it participates ambiguously in the world of romance. Not so much once upon a time as at least twice upon a time, it shifts without apology from the heroic worlds of ancient chronicle to the milieu of erotic intrigue Shakespeare found in Italian Renaissance fiction. And in scenes set in rural Wales, it enters a timeless pastoral world, distant from both heroic and erotic intrigues. The action, confusing to the point of chaos for much of the time, comes to a fusion in a fifth act that is comic in every sense, and at the same time—for those readers, directors, and audiences who agree with Posthumus that it is "a speaking / Such as sense cannot untie"—miraculous.

Like *Pericles,* this play is named for a king, but unlike its predecessor, it departs from its nominal hero for most of its action to focus on his daughter. Imogen commands attention not, like Marina, for the comfort she can bring to the king (although, in the end, she does that too), and not just for the virginal purity she represents, but in her own psychological right. The only heroine of the Romances to adopt, like Rosalind and Viola, the masculine dress that signals the completeness and autonomy unusual in the conventional image of woman, she is even more important in the play's structure than her beloved Posthumus, who for much of the action is hardly worthy of that love. But unlike Rosalind who rules over the ending of her play as Pericles, Cymbeline, Leontes (with Paulina), and Prospero do over the endings of theirs, Imogen finds herself at the end, despite the transformative growth her story allows (especially in a grotesque baptismal image) subjected to her husband like Marina. In one of the most striking images of the play, Posthumus embraces her, and bids her "Hang there like fruit, my soul / Till the tree die" (5.5.263–4).[1]

Imogen's is not the only transformation the complex action unfolds. Posthumus moves from his callow idealism in the first act, through a stage of gullible misogyny, to strong and worthy manhood. Imogen's lost brothers are transformed from rural youths to royal saviors and heirs, the conventions of pastoral confirmed in the strength and sweetness of their actions. Cymbeline himself, prematurely querulous and as unjust as Lear under the evil influence of his second queen, recovers his royal command and magnanimity in the end. The worlds the play reflects—ancient Britain, ancient and contemporary Rome, and the Wales of pastoral retreat—are all transformed when their differences are incorporated and harmonized in the *pax Romana* of the closing lines: "Never was a war did cease / (Ere bloody hands were wash'd) with such a peace."

Date, Text, and Sources

In the absence of definitive evidence, scholarly consensus puts the composition of *Cymbeline* somewhere in the years 1608–11 and suggests that parts of this play may have been written concurrently with *The Winter's Tale,* with which it interconnects in suggestive ways.[2] The first performance for which we have secure evidence was in 1611; publication waited (not unnaturally for a play "owned" by the author's company, the King's Men, in a day of weak copyright protection) until the Folio edition of 1623.

The Folio text, upon which all others are based, is a good one. It is based either on a promptbook incorporating most of the company's stage directions or on a careful transcription of Shakespeare's own working papers, which, toward the end of his life in London, made fuller use of stage directions than those for the early plays.

The interwoven stories of the play derive from a number of sources. Before proceeding to conventional literary models, it is worth recalling that Jonathan Goldberg, David Bergeron, and others have recently found in the royal family of James I an analogue to the ruling families in which the Romances locate their happy endings.[3] Although the contemporary sense of national felicity was to prove short-lived, Shakespeare's England saw James as a quasi-savior for bringing a consort and clear heirs to a succession too often in question under a good, but virgin, queen. Like Cymbeline, James had one daughter and two sons, and, like him in act 5, was an avowed proponent of peace among nations. James's queen, of course (slowly gaining public sympathy as some of his peculiarities became obvious), bears no relation to the wicked stepmother. No claims are made by the new historicists for rigid parallels; they argue only that current history was one of the intertexts contributing to the stuff of the Romances.

Holinshed's *Chronicles* (and perhaps the *Mirror for Magistrates*) stand behind the Roman and British history that frames the two family plots; one of the tales in Boccaccio's *Decameron* and (or) the prose tale in English of

Frederyke of Jennen that repeats the same story stand behind the wager story set in Renaissance Italy; and perhaps an old romantic drama, *The Rare Triumphs of Love and Fortune,* performed at the Elizabethan court a couple of decades earlier, stands behind the story of Belarius and the princes. But, as J. M. Nosworthy comments, "It would be unwise to attach too much weight to [the] parallel features" that link *Cymbeline* to the old play since "these are part of the stock-in-trade of every writer of romance." In Nosworthy's judgment, whether specific debts to the older play are recognizable, *Cymbeline* as a whole is more concerned with the shape of romance as genre—its miracles, its reconciliations, its happy-ever-afters—than with British history or more realistic wager fictions.

Although it is easy to isolate for discussion the barely coherent strands of the plot, because of the brilliance of the poetry they are experienced in their interconnectedness as the play unfolds. Diction and images form webs of significance as compelling as in any of the great tragedies. More than the poetry works toward integration. The final act, wherein all is brought together at breakneck speed, is recognized even by the play's detractors and satirizers as a technical triumph: we marvel that it all manages to happen as it does.[4]

The miracle of *Cymbeline* as drama is that Shakespeare makes all its tragicomic elements, including the "realism" of the wager fiction, knit themselves with a sense of inevitability into the supernal peace and coherence of romance. Here the playwright is visibly playing deus ex machina, as he will do later in the guise of Prospero, and as he makes the Olympian gods serve within each of the first three Romances. He is intervening in a world "realistically" hell-bent to set all right. This, the Christian testament says, God did once upon a time in events set in Bethlehem, Judea, Jerusalem, Golgotha, and a garden, at the very time when Cymbeline was ruling in Britain.

The complex story will take more time in the telling than the linear, more episodic, story of *Pericles,* but the outline will serve economy in further discussions.

The Story

Act 1   In the first scene two gentlemen outline the situation in Cymbeline's family, which has spread distress throughout ancient Britain. His daughter, Imogen, has rebelliously married Posthumus, his adopted son. The king, enraged, has imprisoned Imogen and banished her new husband. He has yielded to his wicked queen's wish that Imogen be matched to her stupid and belligerent son, Cloten, to consolidate the rule of Britain in their joint hands. (The king's male heirs, two sons, were abducted in infancy twenty years earlier.) The young lovers exchange extravagant words of love and promises of fidelity, with a ring and a bracelet as token, before parting. Cloten bewails Imogen's choice but expects that Cymbeline's favor will eventually permit him to enjoy her. Abroad in Italy, at the house of his father's friend, Philario, Posthumus encounters Iachimo. During a bantering and boastful party, various lovers lay claim and counterclaim to the supremacy of their several mistresses. Iachimo challenges Posthumus, declaring that no woman could match the perfection he claims for his wife. Iachimo wagers 10,000 ducats against the diamond ring Imogen has given Posthumus that he can crack Imogen's fidelity. Thus goaded, Posthumus takes the wager.

The queen, obvious in her evil to Cornelius, a doctor, seeks from him a box of poison. The good Cornelius substitutes a magic "cordial" that will cause a deathlike trance from which the sufferer will awaken renewed and refreshed.

While Imogen is lamenting her separation from her husband, Iachimo arrives carrying a message of introduction from Posthumus. His clever discourse, shifting from innuendo to direct accusations of Posthumus's infidelity, deceives Imogen only briefly. Alerted when he offers himself as occasion of sexual "revenge," she rebuffs him. Claiming now to have been testing her, Iachimo reinstates himself in the trust she was asked to give him by her husband's letter by praising the perfect husband of a perfect wife in rhetoric totally matching her own idealization of her marriage. She agrees to his request that she care for a trunk of valuables, ironically promising to "pawn" her "honour" to protect them.

Act 2   As Imogen retires to sleep, Iachimo emerges from his trunk to take note of the bedchamber's details and of the now-unguarded physical person of Imogen. He notes a birthmark, a "mole cinque-spotted," under her left breast and predicts that his knowledge of this blemish will ensure his success against Posthumus. He steals Posthumus's bracelet from her arm as further evidence of her "infidelity."

The next morning, Cloten, with insultingly lustful banter, engages musicians to sing under Imogen's window. His ensuing crude approaches awaken her angry defenses. She counters his excesses avowing that Posthumus's "mean'st garment" means more to her than a myriad of Clotens.

Iachimo returns to Italy to convince the initially skeptical Posthumus of Imogen's infidelity. Posthumus rails against the vices of all women.

Act 3   In formal parley at the British court, Caius Lucius, ambassador from Augustus Caesar, demands the tribute that Cymbeline's uncle had promised annually to Julius Caesar's Rome. The queen and Cloten usurp Cymbeline's prerogative of reply, refusing angrily for him. He lamely repeats the refusal but shows more courtesy than they to the noble Lucius.

Pisanio reads a letter from the angry Posthumus commanding him to murder Imogen for her "disloyalty." Imogen enters to receive a different letter from Posthumus, directing her to meet him at Milford-Haven in Wales. Despite Pisanio's attempt to dissuade her, she prepares to flee the court.

In Wales, Belarius is introduced with Cymbeline's two abducted sons, Guiderius and Arviragus, whom he has brought up in their pastoral retreat in courtly manners and the arts of war. Belarius tells his "sons" how he was unjustly banished when Cymbeline believed slanderous lies against him. Later, in soliloquy, he reveals the boys' true heritage. Near Milford-Haven, Pisanio is forced to show his own letter to Imogen to save her from direct encounter with Posthumus's fury. He offers to say he has killed her, sending some bloody token in supposed proof to Posthumus. When, unwilling to risk a forced marriage to Cloten upon her "divorce" from the banished Posthumus, Imogen rejects Pisanio's advice to return to court, he proposes that she don male attire and seek to serve the noble Lucius who is coming their way. To protect her further, he gives her the box containing the magic potion, which the queen has persuaded him will cure all ills.

Back at court, Cymbeline takes leave of Lucius, knowing that war will ensue. Pisanio is forced to tell Cloten of Imogen's plans to meet Posthumus at Milford-Haven. Cloten decides to dress himself in Posthumus's clothing, kill Posthumus, and then violate Imogen in "merry . . . revenge" for her taunt about preferring her husband's meanest garment to his own person. Imogen arrives at the cave home of Belarius, meets him with his "sons," and, recognizing their innate nobility, accepts and returns the fraternal affection they declare for her as "Fidele."

In Rome, the senator and tribunes are preparing an attack on Britain.

Act 4   Cloten raves in soliloquy, anticipating revenge and counting on the queen to protect him from the consequences of Cymbeline's anger. Imogen, ill, stays at the cave alone and takes the cordial Pisanio has given her. Guiderius, insultingly challenged by Cloten, defends himself, decapitating his adversary and throwing the head in a stream.

Returning to the cave, Guiderius, Arviragus, and Belarius believe the entranced Imogen dead and perform rituals of mourning. When she awakes alone later beside Cloten's headless body, she "recognizes" it as that of Posthumus and in wild grief anoints herself with its blood and embraces it. Lucius arrives, offering his protection, and as "Fidele" she enters his service.

At court as the Roman forces approach, Cymbeline feels vulnerable in the absence of Imogen and Cloten. Pisanio, calmer, expresses trust in the heavens. In Wales, Guiderius and Arviragus resist Belarius's counsel to flee. To prove their manhood, they will take a stand for Britain against the approaching Romans.

Act 5 Posthumus, repenting his rage, grieves over the "bloody cloth" he holds as token of Imogen's "murder." He decides to take on the clothes of a British peasant to fight against the Romans he has, until now, been accompanying. Disjointed skirmishing follows: Posthumus disarms Iachimo; Cymbeline is captured, then released by Belarius, Guiderius, Arviragus, and Posthumus. Posthumus reports to British lords the heroism of the other three in turning the Romans back at a narrow gap. Passing over his own contribution and seeking death, he surrenders to the British as a Roman.

In prison, Posthumus sees in dream his lost parents and brothers, who tell their stories and pray to Jupiter on his behalf. The god descends and promises happiness through affliction: "Whom best I love I cross." Posthumus wakes, now fearless, to the peril of hanging.

Cymbeline knights Belarius, Guiderius, and Arviragus for their exploits and regrets the absence of the "poor soldier" (Posthumus) who stood with them in battle. Cornelius reports that the queen has died, declaring her hatred for Cymbeline and Imogen and confessing her plots against both.

The Roman prisoners are brought to court, among them Lucius, "Fidele," and Posthumus. The scene is set for all strands of the plot to be knit together. Imogen forces a confession of guilt and remorse from Iachimo. Posthumus rediscovers Imogen, and the brothers rejoice to find their "Fidele" alive again. Once his noble birth has been established, Cymbeline forgives Guiderius for the death of Cloten, as a peasant could never be forgiven. Rejoicing, the king reinstates Imogen and Posthumus in his grace and forgives Belarius and Iachimo. Finally, the victorious Cymbeline completes the peace and harmony by promising Lucius he will resume the promised payment of tribute to Caesar, "from the which / We were dissuaded by our wicked queen." Jupiter will preside over the ratifying festivities.

Ritual and the Uncanny: Cloten

Cymbeline shares with *Pericles* (and the other Romances) in the effects of ritual but in a considerably more complex way. The story of Posthumus takes him, as a *puer aeternus,* through an initiation ritual, but it is less striking, we shall see, than Imogen's initiation into the blood mysteries of womanhood.

Both lovers' ordeals can also be seen as ritual deaths and preludes to new births; both are complicated by the person of Cloten, whose "being here" and death in the pastoral world of Wales makes Belarius marvel at what it "to us portends" (4.2.181–83). A full range of the significances I find in this clownish, yet ominous, figure will emerge by the end of the chapter. We begin with him here as an important nucleus of significance.

In his excesses of bravado and rage, Cloten stands apart from the courtly, superficially civil, world and from the pastoral world into which he intrudes as a grotesque outsider[5]—much as Gower stands apart from the action he never enters. Whereas Gower throws an uncanny external light upon the stories of *Pericles,* Cloten weaves it directly into the web of *Cymbeline.*

We recall two details from Freud's definition of the uncanny: the severed head motif in which Cloten's story ends and—less specifically and more pervasively—the sense that the normally familiar is suddenly unfamiliar and threatening as incestuous feelings come to light.[6]

Since the undefined time that he entered the court with Cymbeline's remarriage to Imogen's wicked stepmother, Cloten has stood as the king's stepson in quasi-fraternal relationship to his daughter, Imogen, and to his adopted son, Posthumus. As projected heir in his mother's schemes, he is a surrogate to the legitimate heirs to the kingdom, the stolen princes. Insofar as Cloten is part of the family circle, his ugly lust for Imogen takes on the threatening tone of incest. This, if we note it, adds another menacing aspect to his villainy, but it has altogether deeper effects when we see certain parallels to the more innocent affections that arise between the perfect Imogen and her perfect foster brother and spouse, Posthumus, and between Imogen as "Fidele" and the young princes, her brothers by both birth and adoption.

We spring rightly to the defense of these good characters, just as we do to those innocents whom the depth psychologists (of many camps) find "incestuous." Feelings, desires, and ideas may come and go in consciousness without being acted upon, and beloved persons who match the enticing outlines of a father or a mother in the lover's unconscious world may be perfectly proper objects of love—as Cloten clearly is not. The object of this current game is not to convict any psyche, within or beyond the fiction, of some wicked mode of "incest" but to explore the uncanny effects Cloten provokes.

The severed head provides the key to the uncanniness we experience and to the interpretation of the starkest rituals of the play. Cloten's head—never much use to him or anyone else before it was detached—leaves behind it the headless body a young wife cannot distinguish from her husband's.

If we allegorize the actions of this play, as Neoplatonic traditions had taught Shakespeare's contemporaries to do, we can start with Imogen's early protestation to her father: "I chose an eagle, / And did avoid a puttock." Cloten comes to stand in a mysterious way for all that idealizing traditions hold in suspicion—for the very earthiness that the eagle flies from in his fascination with the sun, that the base "puttock" assimilates and augments in its role as scavenger, and, if we allow ourselves to ponder an aural pun in Imogen's metaphor, sits heavily upon.

Cloten, we come to see, signifies the body; beheaded, he makes manifest in the action the mind-body split, typical of both Hellenistic and Christian idealisms, that dominates the *puer* type at most stages of his romantic quest. Cloten's closest kinsmen in dramatic history are the wild man of medieval folk festivals and the "old vice" in the miracle and morality plays still performed in the provinces in Shakespeare's youth.[7] All, in some senses, represent the "old Adam" of the flesh with whom, in Christian thinking, all need to come to terms if they are to enter into new and fuller life. To so load Cloten as an allegorical signifier is, of course, to risk depriving him of his abominable idiosyncrasies and risk masking his affinities to another literary type, the *miles gloriosus,* in which he shares with his less despicable brothers, Falstaff and Parolles, and with Spenser's equally ridiculous but less menacing Braggadocchio. Nonetheless, the risk of interpreting Cloten primarily as body must be taken if we are to come to understand what his presence, in Belarius's word, "portends."

As we move now away from Cloten to discuss relatively minor characters and issues in the play, we should be prepared to find that the relationship and response of any character to Cloten will help us to define that character, much as responses to the devil in earlier drama separate the sheep from the goats. For the allegorist, of course, all persons are defined by their responses to embodied evil.

Threats to Social Order: Credulity, Power in Woman, and Slander

Although Cymbeline holds the throne throughout the play, secure rule is established in the kingdom of Britain only at the end, and then only under the benign aspect of the transcendent ruler, Jupiter. Earlier actions in the national and family plots are dominated by the evil and divisive scheming of the queen to put her unworthy son on the throne through Imogen's bed and in the central love plot by the similarly evil and divisive scheming of Iachimo. By such machinations, good characters are thwarted in their predominantly positive intentions and are forced not to act but to react, or remain passive. In this, an ironist will see, they differ little from most persons of good intention in any far from perfect world.

Yet merely to react is no virtue in a ruler. Although nothing suggests that Cymbeline either deliberately chose, or having chosen, consciously countenances, evil in his queen, we find that he lets himself off too easily when he asks, "Who is't can read a woman" (5.5.48), and speaks of his error as folly (5.5.67). High-minded and well-meaning rulers do singular harm if they make no judicious effort to read circumstances beyond superficial appearances. The errors of rulers lead to chaos in the body politic. Until the knitting up of the final scene, this play manifests a progressive disintegration of social order in both nation and family. To explain, if not to excuse, Cymbeline's "folly," it derives from his need for a new family after losing both male heirs by abduction and their mother to death. (Both losses had an antecendent cause—the king's unjust response to slander, to which we shall soon turn.)

Posthumus, by conventional understanding head and ruler of the new family unit he and Imogen have forged by their secret marriage, stands under the same judgment as Cymbeline for one major error: that of the credulity that exposes him to manipulation and forces him to react rather than to control his actions. Admittedly, by the forbidden wedding, Posthumus has transgressed against order in both family and state. But guided by the First Gentleman in the first scene—"he that . . . married her . . . is a creature" without equal; "I do not think / So fair an outward, and such stuff within / Endows a man but he"—we do not judge him harshly at first but absolve him sympathetically. When a foolish and tyrannous ruler proves himself unworthy, rebellious actions are defensible in our postmedieval judgment. At least Posthumus's transgression has been an action, one suited to a strong young lover.

Our opinions change radically once the wager plot begins to unfold. The husband who has promised to "remain / The loyal'st . . . that did e'er plight troth" (1.2,26–27) weakly submits to manipulation. Not only does he engage in a party game that poises the virtue he boasts in his unparalleled bride against Iachimo's gold, he throws into the balance the diamond ring he has accepted from Imogen in lieu and as token of the "embracements" (1.2.47) the king's ire has prevented them from enjoying. The language and symbolism of the wager scene (1.5) turn Imogen, quite clearly, into her husband's possession, one he risks undervaluing and parting with far too easily. When Iachimo returns with "evidence" of Imogen's "stain" in the bracelet he has stolen and the report of the "mole, right proud / Of [its] most delicate lodging" under her breast (2.4.134–36), Posthumus caves in easily, wildly joining in accusations against this particular, and then against all, women. The husband stands guilty of compliance in the face of a wily villainy he makes no real effort to "read." His failure to defend his wife under attack parallels Cymbeline's failure to defend his daughter against the queen's, and Cloten's, assaults. Credulity, the obverse of virtuous trust in situations that do not justify trust, weakens them both. So does the irrational anger that both turn in emasculated frustration on the innocent victim of their weakness. Imogen, victimized first by their passive reactions to evil, is then subject to their perverse resorts to "action": Cymbeline imprisons her, mildly enough, it seems, when we compare that bondage to Posthumus's wild threats to "tear her limb-meal!" (2.4.147) and his subsequent order for her murder.

We turn now from credulity to another threat to social order: the unseemly usurpation of power by a woman. Cymbeline's queen resembles the wicked Dionyza in her unfeminine lust for power and in the unscrupulous means she is willing to employ to gain it. Both are driven by perverse maternal eros focused on hope for a child. To scheme for a child's advantageous marriage may seem, under conventions that deny a more direct exercise of power to women, forgivable in a mother—but not when the motive leads to murder. Obviously there are limits to the social power a woman (as wife and mother) may seek to exercise.

When she goes beyond acceptable limits, the queen resembles that feared figure of folktale and nightmare, the wicked witch. Her transparently false denial marks her as such in her first speech: "you shall not find me, daughter, / After the slander of most stepmothers, / Evil-ey'd to you" (1.2.1–3). Imogen is not deceived, nor are we. Witches, of course, are traditionally feared for the "evil eye" that destroys health and harmony. As a dabbler in physic, this black witch is diametrically opposed to the white magician—in this play, Cornelius, who wisely thwarts her schemes; in *Pericles,* Cerimon, who revives Thaisa. (White magic in *The Tempest* is the sphere of Prospero, who seeks to heal his society therewith; and in *The Winter's Tale,* of Paulina—a good countertype to the queen.)

The power hunger of the witch-woman or wicked mother in the Romances often needs a male agent to satisfy it. Dionyza, who feigns her wifely submission to the well-meaning but impotent Cleon, needs Leonine, whose name befits and extends her regal ferocity, to carry out her murderous plan. In *Cymbeline,* the queen, by encouraging her son's unseemly ambition and lust, turns Cloten from laughable bumbler to murderous lout and looses him into the hitherto sheltered and innocent world of Wales to wreak the damage she, as woman, cannot accomplish directly. She also, by giving Pisanio the box of "poison" we know to be less deadly than she thinks, tries (as Posthumus does also) to make that good servant her instrument in murder. That the ruse has the uncannily good effects we discuss later does not soften her evil; it inspires us, rather, to marvel at the power of providence (working through good healer and good servant) to bring ultimate good out of such vicious actions.

In the international plot also, we see the queen manipulating men to work her destructive will. The battles between the Britons and the Romans need never have marred the peace: the accord between the nations, says Holinshed, had been such that Cymbeline was fostered in the court of Augustus, much as Posthumus has been brought up in this own.[8] Shakespeare's audiences would not have seen ancient Rome as an enemy, although the stereotype of Iachimo's modern Italy as corrupt was another matter. James I even encouraged comparisons of himself to Augustus, uniter of nations, consolidator of peace. The national myth, advanced by the Tudor chroniclers and embraced by Tudor and Stuart monarchs alike, located the origins of ancient Britain in "Brut," who came from Rome to extend one empire and stayed to found another. The harmony of *Cymbeline*'s ending, then, would have been perfectly consistent with good rule throughout the time span of this ancient fiction: the war over tribute was the evil result of monstrous female interference by the queen in her husband's responsibilities.

For another serious threat to social order, I turn now to a word the queen first introduces in the play, "slander." This criminal misuse of language to undercut the social position of its victim was much feared at Elizabethan and Stuart courts. Spenser had projected it into the horrid figure of the multitongued Blatant Beast, still on the rampage in faeryland when *The Faerie Queene* breaks off. All persons of privilege, if neither totally virtuous nor totally tyrannous and powerful, have reason to fear the language that can undermine privilege by appearing to justify its elimination. Accusations that are true, being mere language, can be countered by claims that they are false. This the queen illustrates when she projects, in a way typical of evildoers, her own sins upon hypothetical persons who "slander . . . most stepmothers" (1.2.1–3). Not only is the devil father of the lies of projection—so are his disciples.

Slander, with other false and perverse uses of language, constitutes the strongest of threats to all social orders that are founded on trust and to all social actions based in trust. Trust within a nation is based on assumptions of the loyalty of all subjects to a worthy king; trust between nations is based on the virtue of the leaders of nations as it issues in their respect for the bonds of treaties. Within the family, mutual trust between spouses, and between parents and children, is the originating and sustaining social bond. When trust is breached, either by insufficient faith or by insufficient merit in any one member, the most basic of social structures will crumble. Slander is that misuse of language that, by imputing lack of merit to a ruler, lays the basis for rebellion or, by falsely accusing the hierarchically inferior, lays the basis for an unjust judgment by the ruler.

Slander, preying and depending on credulity, drives two of the actions in *Cymbeline,* the wager plot and the abduction plot. In the latter, Belarius explains (3.3.55–73), the bonds between ruler and courtier were broken by stages: slander was spoken; slander was too easily believed. The honorable victim of slander, reacting to his ruler's breach of faith, breached faith in return—following an ancient masculine code of revenge—by stealing away the sons of the king, guarantors of stability in the kingdom. The order of the kingdom was broken by something as insubstantial, and as powerful in the absence of vigilant judgment, as false words.

Belarius would never have abducted the princes had not "two villains, whose false oaths prevail'd / Before my perfect honour" sworn he was "confederate with the Romans" (3.3.66–68).[9] The villains, unnamed, have presumably vanished during the intervening twenty years. Their villainy, introduced here to be dropped but for brief mention in the resolution scene, means little to the present plot but much in the interrelated themes of the play.

The villains misused language in two ways: by telling slanderous falsehoods and by swearing to them. The king was doubly duped: he believed the falsehoods, and he accepted "false oaths" before the "perfect honour" of the accused Belarius. Here, as in *Pericles,* the New Testament stands as intertext: good men should "swear not at all" but interact in basic trust.[10] That Belarius to that time had deserved trust, and was denied it under slander, all but justifies his theft of the children: the original breach in the social order was none of his doing.

The slander against Belarius has deserved this much emphasis primarily because it provides the background for discussing the much more important issue of the slander against Imogen in the wager plot. Belarius's vengeful response provides a masculine contrast to Imogen's saintly and feminine forbearance under a provocation as grave as his.

The conventions differentiating masculine from feminine honor have always located the former in the bonds governing men's actions in a social hierarchy: honor involves loyally serving and defending king and country and speaking truth in such service. A less authentic, but not inconsiderable, source of public honor for a man lies in what he possesses. Great wealth, or the possession of anything else desirable in the eyes of other men, enhances a man's status. Of course, truly honorable men, like King Simonides, know better than to judge the inward man by outward possessions. Still, if the possession is a woman, not a splendid display of armor, clothing, or jewels, her virtue may realistically reflect on his. The metaphoric use, common in the Renaissance, of such words as *treasure* and *ornament* in reference to women of moral virtue underscores the points I am making here.[11]

A woman's position is different from a man's. Although she can share vicariously in her father's honor before marriage, or her husband's after, her honor as a person rests primarily in the sexual purity for which she is most valued in a society dominated by men. If unmarried, she must keep her reputation unsullied for the sake of her father's. He is judged by his control over the women of his household; his social and financial status are threatened by any action that would devalue a daughter on the marriage market. If she is married, her honor (located now not in celibate inexperience but in fidelity to the marriage vows) is all important to her husband's honor. Although in the masculine world of politics a man's service to the ruler outweighs more private concerns, personal reputation will be weighed in the balance with service.[12]

The most grievous slander against a woman, then, will be directed against her sexual purity—just as that same purity, if unsullied, will tempt her husband to boastfulness. We can begin to see how the issues of trust, fidelity, false language, and the ability as interpreter of language to discern the true from the false interconnect in the fabric of this play. Before we take up these issues in reference to Posthumus and Imogen, we turn to a few of the less fully developed characters.

Pisanio, Lucius, Belarius, and the Princes

Pisanio's function cuts across all plots. Posthumus's servant initially, he is left to serve and protect Imogen on her husband's departure when he becomes the one person she can trust in a court dominated by her wicked stepmother. If this were totally a fairy tale, Pisanio's role might be that of the fairy godmother. There is a touch of magic (unwitting on his part) in the fact that Pisanio conveys to his charge the magic potion that heals through seeming to kill. Without him, Imogen would have missed her crucial baptismal ritual.

Pisanio's major function is as a model of the trustworthy courtier-servant. When his master commands him to murder, he has the courage, unlike Thaliard but like Camillo in *The Winter's Tale,* to thwart an unworthy order. (Of course, Posthumus, even mad with rage, hardly represents the threat of an absolute villain like Antiochus.)

Pisanio also, by ensuring for "Fidele" the protection of Lucius when he can protect her no longer, serves to endorse the virtue of the Romans. His integrity by that point is so unquestionable that the audience is made ready to accept Cymbeline's abrupt change on the matter of the tribute. The honor of Lucius, the only Roman to be given any individuality, already signaled by the courtesy Cymbeline shows him, is furthered by Pisanio's trust. The virtue of Lucius, established in our eyes by Pisanio, contributes credibility to the supernal peace of the final scene.

Lucius has one scene that humanizes him, even as it adds one more testimony to Imogen's universal charm. After he has been taken by the British, has begged that "Fidele," "a Briton born," be ransomed and freed, and has watched the "boy" find favor in the eyes of Cymbeline, he quite understandably expects that "Fidele's" loyalty to "his" Roman master will lead to intercession for Lucius. But the "boy," granted one "boon" only by the king, announces regretfully "other work in hand"—the redemption of Posthumus who has been brought to court in bonds. Lucius laments, "The boy disdains me, / He leaves me, scorns me" and finds it a lesson to all that depend on "the truth of girls and boys," hinting at an affection beyond that a master need feel for a page. He seems, in the final phrase, to have penetrated Imogen's disguise. The effect taints neither her nor him. Rather, it adds its contribution to the effect of universal love and harmony that is building throughout the scene.

Belarius, the next character to consider, is essential to the plot of the lost princes. We have seen already how, as victim of slander, his story reinforces the motif of slander against Imogen and demonstrates the destructive force of false language in a state, as in more personal alliances.

As protector and nurturer of the innocent princes, Belarius, after his initial act of abduction, represents the feminine quality of nurturing. In the final scene he even speaks of himself in female terms—"pay me for the nursing of thy sons"—although he goes on to indicate that he had taken into banishment Euriphile, the boys' nurse (since dead), "whom for the theft I wedded." Belarius also shows a feminine side when, as the Romans approach, he urges his "sons" to flee with him to the high mountains to escape danger. This is no cowardice. When the young princes demonstrate that they have assimilated the ideals their "father" has presented to them in heroic tales, Belarius shows himself fully capable of heroic action. Together they ward off the Romans at the pass.

In sum, Belarius presents a well-rounded image of manhood. Long held in sympathy by the audience as a victim of injustice, he is fully absolved and reinstated politically in the reconciliation scene. His ready acceptance by Cymbeline indicates the king's recognition of his own contribution to the split in the body politic, as much as his approval of Belarius's military valor.

The final function of this courtier, then, is to confirm in action the genuine transformation in the character of the king.

The young princes, Guiderius and Arviragus by birth but in exile "Polydore" and "Cadwal" to Belarius's "Morgan," play to perfection the roles of romance heroes. Their images emphasize the degree to which Posthumus departs from the romance hero by his actions in the wager plot. Clean, sturdy, heroic in behavior when the invasion of Britain engages the noble instincts that are theirs by both nature and nurture, the princes already hold the affectionate respect of the audience when the turns of plot reveal them to be Cymbeline's lost heirs.

One of the means by which that revelation is confirmed both likens Guiderius to, and distinguishes him from, his royal sister. He had "upon his neck a mole, a sanguine star," his father remembers, and such a "natural stamp" indeed the elder prince bears. Imogen, we know, has such a birthmark—the "mole cinque-spotted: like the crimson drops / I' th' bottom of a cowslip" to which Iachimo's lascivious description testifies. The similarities are obvious: both marks are moles, the male's is "sanguine" and the female's is marked by crimson drops that suggest blood. But the prince's is on his neck—a bodily blemish placed symbolically on the bridge that links the body to the head, seat of the ruling spirit.[13] The princess's is lower, under her feminine breast, a position as suspect in its eroticism as the cup-shaped blossom of the cowslip to whose spots the "crimson drops" are likened. The blemish on the male confirms his right to rule; the blemish on the female convinces her bridegroom of her unfitness as his "perfect" bride. A modern woman, seeing in the birthmarks the double standard in the different plot strands, wonders whether to credit Shakespeare with conscious awareness of the imbalance in the scales of sexual justice or simply to credit a poetic genius with constructing a symbolic pattern so universal to patriarchal cultures that it can be turned to advantage in feminist argument. I suspect the latter and applaud the rightness of Shakespeare's symbolic structure, whether conscious or not. A mole can confirm a man in power; any such spot on a woman will be taken as a sign of moral imperfection.[14]

The affection of the princes for Imogen is another issue. "Incestuous" in the best sense of depth psychology, it is indicative of the original harmony of the family circle and of the "omnipotence" that only an innocent and happy baby can feel before the inevitable separation from nurturing mother. The affection may also titillate the audience both as it suggests forbidden aspects of brother-sister love and as it extends the sexual ambiguities of cross-dressing on the Elizabethan and Jacobean stage, where the women's roles were always played by young male actors.[15] What ultimately is forbidden in a fallen world is the recovery of original perfection. We sons and daughters of Adam and Eve can never hope to enjoy unbroken harmony with another for long; we have been expelled at our origin from the Edenic harmony of life in the womb.

The princes serve another function: their reemergence at court cancels the political impediment to Imogen's marriage with Posthumus, which was never inappropriate in personal terms until Posthumus abandoned faith. It was only "wrong" politically because those with usurped power—the queen and her son—needed the heir to the kingdom in an alliance more advantageous to themselves.

When the youths promise upon meeting "Fidele" to love her as a brother, Imogen testifies to their goodness in her eyes—"would it had been so, that they / Had been my father's sons"—as well as to her awareness that "then had my prize / Been less, and so more equal ballasting / To thee, Posthumus" (3.7.48–51). The family reunion in the final scene does not, as her father suggests, so much lose her a kingdom (5.5.374) as gain her "two worlds" (5.5.374–75): that of her family and that in which she may enjoy her husband unopposed.

The reestablishment of her family sets the stage for Imogen's happy ending, just as Posthumus's vision of his family prepares for his. But before the social consummation of their happiness in reunion, each young lover must undergo a transforming initiation ritual.

The *Puer* and the Virgin Again: The Quests of Imogen and Posthumus

We can now trace the stories of the young lovers of this Romance, finding in their language and their actions signs to the larger patterns of life into which Shakespeare is incorporating them and initiating us. Since they have been married before the play begins, and all that happens to either eventually affects the other, I shall separate their stories only where the action keeps them apart for a time.

They begin their lives together as beautiful, publicly admired, parentally opposed, young idealists—not unlike the tragic Romeo and Juliet. Each sees in the other the perfect mate, and the perfection they admire is that of the spirit, symbolized in Posthumus by Imogen's metaphor for him, the "eagle," and in Imogen by Posthumus's exaltation of her chastity above that of the goddess Diana. (Iachimo recalls that praise in 5.5.179–81.) Other characters reinforce the images of perfection they ascribe to each other. The two gentlemen describing Posthumus in the opening scene almost run out of superlatives: as a boy he took to learning "as we do air . . . / And in's spring became a harvest"[16]; he lives now "most prais'd, most lov'd"; and "to his mistress . . . her own price / Proclaims how she esteem'd him." The praise of the husband flows naturally into the praise of the bride: her worth—"price"—is the measure of his. Both are paragons.

Imogen's praise is sung not only by Posthumus but, however wryly, by Iachimo when he first sets eyes on her: "All of her that is out of door most rich! / If she be furnish'd with a mind so rare, She is alone th' Arabian bird; and I / Have lost the wager" (1.7.15–18). In the poetic pattern emerging, Imogen is a bird more exalted than the eagle she sees in Posthumus and, rarer, a phoenix. Both birds, in tradition, are perfect enough to have been associated with Christ: the sun-seeking eagle as the symbol of his beloved disciple, John, and the fiery phoenix—in its uniqueness, its self-immolation and its miraculous resurrection—as one of many symbols for Christ Himself.

Aspiring to the highest—in their images of themselves as they reflect the admiration of others, and in their beloveds—both Imogen and Posthumus are caught up in incestuous narcissism. In the one who has been until lately brother (or sister) in the royal household, Imogen (or Posthumus) sees a reflection of the perfect self she (or he) has been led by privilege and admiration to believe in. Like Narcissus, each has fallen in love with a reflection of the self. Unlike that of Narcissus, their illusory reflections are not found in the mirror of a pool, but are projected on persons as like their youthful selves as noble birth and an upbringing in the same family can ensure.

Caught in idealism and illusion, Posthumus and Imogen are caught also in the web of language—that projection, and that shaper, of the highest human aspirations and capacities. As Posthumus begins to take his leave upon banishment, he reveals much to us: "My queen, my mistress / . . . weep no more, lest I give cause / To be suspected of more tenderness / Than does become a man." His courtly address repeats the possessive *my* that we noticed in Pericles' addresses to his consort, and the weeping he forbids is feared not as it expresses the lady's sorrow but as it potentially subverts his own masculine image. He goes on: "I will remain / The loyal'st husband that did e'er plight troth," his words revealing the self-reflexive movement of his thinking. He is like Shakespeare's young Troilus here, more than a little in love with the image his words project of himself as faithful lover. The loyalty of both youths, spun of words, proves fragile under test. As Troilus concedes without protest that his Cressida must be passed over to the Greek camp where on arrival she will suffer the humiliation of the kissing game, so Posthumus concedes victory in the wager to Iachimo without responsibly trying to read his perfidious actions. Imogen, in contrast, suspects Iachimo's motives very early, until her suspicions are allayed by the hyperbolic praise of her beloved that matches her own, still adolescent, idealizations.

Imogen can be as captivated by her own words as by the words of another—whether her husband's, Iachimo's, or Pisanio's. When the latter brings news of Posthumus's departure by sea, she savors first her image of a waving handkerchief and a Posthumus on the ship gradually shrinking "till he had melted from / The smallness of a gnat, to air" (1.4.8–21). Then she turns her attention more fully on her grieving self: "I did not take my leave of him, but had / Most pretty things to say: . . . / How I would think on him at certain hours, / Such thoughts, and such" (1.4.25–28). She seems to be mourning the loss of opportunity for her own verbal performance more than the loss of her husband.

In these early stages of their love, Posthumus and Imogen are like any adolescent moving from self-love, through the love of the self's perfect image in another, toward the fuller love that forgets self in total acceptance of the less than perfect other. When their loves remain arrested at the level of narcissistic projection and language, the young lovers are not themselves totally to blame:

> or ere I could
> Give him that parting kiss, which I had set
> Betwixt two charming words, comes in my father,
> And like the tyrannous breathing of the north,
> Shakes all our buds from growing.
> (1.4.33–37)

Imogen's complaint against Cymbeline, however revealing of her own self-dramatization, tells the audience much more: their love is merely in bud, although the plural, "buds," speaks of the range of potentiality in that love. They have had no time to grow together, no time probably to consummate the marriage physically. Two scenes earlier, when Imogen has prettily given her mother's diamond to her husband, commanding him to "keep it till you woo another wife / When Imogen is dead," the young husband has exclaimed, "How, how? Another? / You gentle gods, give me but this I have . . .!" (1.2.44–46).

It would be, I suppose, possible to interpret that speech simply as a fervent prayer to remain together, if we do not remember other evidence. But Posthumus's boasts about his lady's chastity seem to have been founded on his experience of her continent behavior toward him more than on his imagination of her behavior toward others. When he thinks she has yielded to Iachimo, his ravings reflect sexual frustration as well as jealousy and the pain of losing the ideal image of womanhood he has projected on her. He raves against all women, now he thinks the one he has believed perfect to be flawed:

> my mother seem'd
> The Dian of that time: so doth my wife
> The nonpareil of this. O vengeance, vengeance!
> Me of my lawful pleasure she restrain'd,
> And pray'd me oft forbearance: did it with
> A pudency so rosy, the sweet view on't
> Might well have warm'd old Saturn; that I thought her
> As chaste as unsunn'd snow.
>
> (2.4.158–65)

The last line hints that the cold purity of the lady has yet to be melted by a symbolic sun—the parallel in the hierarchy of the skies to the eagle in the bird kingdom, and in the animal, to the lion that Posthumus Leonatus bears in his name. The hint is strengthened by Iachimo's later testimony: "He spoke of her, as Dian had hot dreams, / And she alone were cold" (1.5.180–81).

It is reasonable to assume that the marriage, contracted in secret, has not been consummated before Posthumus's departure—partly because Imogen, with an adolescent virgin's idealistic apprehensions concerning sexuality, has managed to postpone the "embracements" that the equally idealistic, but more pressingly ardent, young husband has been seeking. The image of "unsunn'd snow" becomes the ground of innocence against which the patterns of blood initiation for both lovers are set.

We first see Imogen directly rebuffing male desires when the suitor is Cloten. Any other response to him would be unthinkable, even if she had not already married her ideal counterpart, Posthumus. Cloten's very name suggests his unsuitability. If we give the "o" a short sound, it reminds us of clods and clots—earthy, bloody, low. If we give it a long "o," it sounds like the clothing by which the rascal seeks to take on a worthier appearance and suggests the hollowness, or worse, of a character who must hide behind external garments. Either pronunciation will return us to the sense that we are to read Cloten as, in some way, "body."

We hear only later, in act 2, that Imogen has also been "restraining" the "lawful pleasure" of her wedded, idealized, beloved. She will come to value his body only when, resurrected from her own apparent bodily death, she awakes to see her husband's garments on the bloody headless trunk of his foster brother and takes the body to be his. The "buds" of her desire, so long deferred by romantic words and dreams, burst into flower in the hideous embrace that bloodily baptizes her into full conjugal love.

The scene has embarrassed many, who have felt they have stumbled upon naked perversity, and many have sought to deny the embarrassment by criticizing what they consider an awkward and excessive application of the romance convention of mistaken identity.[17] Although the beheading and its consequences may seem a little excessive, as well as uncanny, Shakespeare takes some pains to make Imogen's mistake believable. When Lucius arrives to find her in a dead faint across the body he exclaims, "Soft ho, what trunk is here? / Without his top? The ruin speaks that sometime / It was a worthy building" (4.2.353–55). Clearly Cloten was not misshapen, however deformed his moral character. Without the head, one strong young male body can be mistaken for another, especially if the observer is just awaking from a drug-induced swoon and has earlier had her loving attention directed primarily toward things of the spirit.

A careful reading of Imogen's distracted words in act 4, scene 2 (291–332) will trace the pattern of her initiation. Waking to the withered flowers with which her new brothers and their "father" have adorned her supposed bier, she cries:

> These flowers are like the pleasures of the world;
> This bloody man, the care on't. I hope I dream:
> For so I thought I was a cave-keeper,
> And cook to honest creatures. But 'tis not so.

In her brief pastoral life, Imogen, however disguised, has moved contentedly into the role of homemaker to her adopted family, two of whom she recognizes instinctively as kin. This rough awakening separates her from the comfortable life she has found, a life far better than the horror that she knew when she learned from Pisanio that slander had moved the husband of her romantic dreams to a woman-hating, murderous rage: "I must be ripp'd:—to pieces with me!—O, / Men's vows are women's traitors!" (3.4.53–54). At that stage she would willingly have died: "Do thou thy master's bidding . . . Look, / I draw the sword myself, take it and hit . . . my heart: / Fear not, 'tis empty of all things but grief" (3.4.65–69). After the interlude in which she has come to peace in a role that usually follows, by extended time, the dreams of adolescence, and after the swoon, which as a little death signals the transition to yet another mode of consciousness, she wakes again to horror:

> The dream's here still: even when I wake it is
> Without me as within me: not imagin'd, felt.
> A headless man? The garments of Posthumus?
> I know the shape of's leg: this is his hand:
> His foot Mercurial; his Martial thigh:
> The brawns of Hercules: But his Jovial face—
> Murder in heaven! How?—'Tis gone . . .

Piteously, she shows where her affection has been anchored:

> O Posthumus, alas,
> Where is thy head? where's that? Ay me! where's that?
> Pisanio might have killed thee at the heart,
> And left this head on.

She finds "pregnant, pregnant" the fact that Pisanio gave her the cordial she has found "murderous to her senses." Her metaphoric use of the word *pregnant* shows that she is moving toward realization of all that the loss of her husband will deny her.

When she cries, "Give colour to my pale cheek with thy blood" the text directs actress and director to stage the ritual of a baptism in blood, which, "horrid" and uncanny, will move the audience to levels of awareness that idealizing language does not reach. That dramatic experience signifies more than a mere bodily initiation. Imogen has already shown more magnanimity, and a more "feminine" passivity, than her mate in reacting without desire for revenge to his breach of faith. Now, in the bloody embrace, she accepts and "loves" the headless body without any thought of the "perfection" she earlier identified with "the head"—without any thought whatsoever of its deserving. Such love, in its total generosity, is akin to the love of God that in gospel story also uses the vehicle of a bloody human body to communicate itself to the world.[18]

"The transformation mysteries of the woman are primarily blood-transformation mysteries that lead her to the experience of her own creativity and produce a numinous impression upon the man," says Erich Neumann.[19] Like most other male theorists of his generation, Neumann ascribes little spiritual potential to the woman and takes a more limited view of woman's range of creativity than I can sanction. Yet since here we are scrutinizing another text generated by a sympathetic but undeniably masculine consciousness, this insight is apt. Imogen is awakening to the experience that will initiate her into full acceptance of the carnal aspects of her love.

Neumann points us toward the most uncanny and numinous turn in Posthumus's initiation process. "Yea, bloody cloth, I'll keep thee: for I wish'd / Thou shouldst be colour'd thus," says Posthumus in soliloquy as the fifth act opens. Clutching the "bloody sign" Pisanio has sent, he muses:

> You married ones,
> If each of you should take this course, how many
> Must murder wives much better than themselves
> For wrying but a little?
>
> (5.1.2–5)

Far from "unconvincing" as Nosworthy finds it,[20] the remorse strikes home when we see this scene as a ritual paralleling Imogen's blood mystery. Posthumus has been transformed by the "bloody cloth," an object fully familiar to the sexually mature woman but alienatingly other to a youthful, inexperienced male. Posthumus, mourning over the tangible sign of the bodily death of his wife, forgets the rage he felt as romantic *puer* in love with an image of perfection. The supposed infidelity that shattered the image he now sees (it has not yet been disproved to him) as "wrying but a little"—so much less grievous than his own that the wife is "much better" than he.

Like Imogen, Posthumus has been moved by the supposed death of the other to value the real person, body and all, abandoning the idealism that has made them both easy prey to slander. The contrast with a similar symbol in *Othello* confirms this understanding. In the tragedy, the handkerchief spotted with embroidered strawberries becomes, by Iago's slanderous villainy, the "ocular proof" Othello has demanded of Desdemona's infidelity.[21] Iachimo's very name enforces the parallel to Iago's slanderous villainy, suggesting that Shakespeare is revising the outlines of the tragedy for the comic ending of this Romance. Othello's token provokes the murder of a wife "much better" than himself, whom he comes to see too late as a pearl of innocence. This cloth, similarly spotted with red, moves Posthumus conversely to recognize that love does not depend on perfection in the beloved. Because Pisanio's virtue has prevented him from executing the murder, Posthumus's remorse comes in time.

Posthumus's participation in the mystery of Imogen's "death" prepares him for his own. No more than she can he in his turn wish to live without his beloved. He seeks "th' sure physician, Death" when he surrenders to the British as a Roman, and in such self-abandon he is ready for the dream of his lost parents and brothers that, supplying what he has always lacked, confirms at last his sense of selfhood.[22]

To put it in more Jungian terms, the *puer,* having moved to the full acceptance of a woman he believes less than perfect, is rewarded in his new maturity by the vision that tells him the family stories that he, as posthumous child, has never before been able to hear. The blood ritual has tipped his psyche away from self-protecting animus to self-abandoning anima; the vision of male and female parents is needed to bring the two back into balance. With this focus we see the Jupiter who appears on the eagle in response to the parents' invocation as the power of command in Posthumus's now realized self.[23] Since Jupiter is merely the chief in a polytheistic pantheon, his presence suggests, realistically, that other gods, other powers in the self, may yet return to assert themselves as this major transformation in life yields place to others more minor.[24] So it is, when the masculine force of psyche dominates again in the ending as Posthumus, in "Hang there like fruit," reveals his, and his author's, patriarchal bias.

As yet we have considered the appearance of Jupiter in Posthumus's dream only from the point of view of a character within the fiction. Now we step back out of the fiction and look at Jupiter from the point of view of the audience or reader.

Jupiter as Deus Ex Machina

However a given director chooses to mount this fourth scene of the final act, the stage directions make it clear that Shakespeare is calling for impressive spectacle: "Jupiter descends in thunder and lightning, sitting upon an eagle: he throws a thunderbolt. The Ghosts fall on their knees." In the Jacobean theater, Jupiter must have remained on the upper stage, having descended "ex machina"—on some technical device—from the theatrical superstructure.[25] Not only the ghosts would be thunderstruck. The audience would share their awe, as modern audiences still can whenever the director works to develop the sense of miracle. On stage Jupiter is as visibly present as Posthumus: the audience will easily forget (or perhaps never fully realize) that the vision represents an inner world. In response to human invocation, a god is showing himself, explaining his decrees and intentions, prophesying Posthumus's happy future directly, and the "fortunate" future of Britain in the enigmatic "tablet" he lays upon the breast of the sleeping hero.

This deus ex machina, true to his dramatic lineage, prepares us for all the happy tumbling together of events in the rest of the act. When in the fiction a god can answer human call and intervene in human lives, why shouldn't a playwright, god to his creation, intervene at will to bring about this happy ending? Comedy, one playwright has told us, "is an escape, not from truth but from despair: a narrow escape into faith. It believes in a universal cause for delight, even though knowledge of the cause is always twitched away from under us, which leaves us to rest on our own buoyancy."[26] The audience's resultant "faith" bears no relation whatsoever to divisive creeds or other verbal formulations of intellectual belief. It is a deeper, more pervasive matter of feeling, of joyful apprehension. No matter what the tragic potential in life's circumstances (and every life will end in death), that apprehension of a "cause for delight" that comedy gives us buoys us up when a Jupiter disappears, when the closing of the curtain ushers us out of the theater. If our participation in the mimeses of theater has been full enough, it may buoy us up still when we wake to an ordinary day.[27]

Some of the words this Jupiter speaks evoke Christian reverberations: "Whom best I love I cross" summons the memory of "whom the Lord loveth he chasteneth" (Heb. 12:6), and tellingly, in "cross," the memory of the ultimate instrument of chastening. His comforting words to the parents, "Be content, / Your low-laid son our godhead will uplift . . . Our Jovial star reigned at his birth," do not, of course, refer to the baby and the star of Bethlehem—they precede "and in / Our temple was he married" to the "lady Imogen." But the echoes of the gospel stories, anticipating the reiterated references to a supernal peace at the end of the act, serve to remind us that the chronicle of Cymbeline is situated in history at the same time as the birth of another "low-laid son," the Prince of Peace.

Shakespeare is never doctrinaire. If we are to learn from him at all, it will be by accepting the signs that point to something no one text, whether dramatic or traditionally sacred, can confine—to a universal ground for joy that has much to do with human love.

Chapter Four

"By law and process of great nature . . . free'd": *The Winter's Tale*

Just as all of the Romances move beyond the toughness of the tragedies without leaving tragic potentialities behind, so each Romance reaches beyond its predecessor in certain ways. If we see in *Pericles* a skeletal paradigm of the unrealistic conventions of romance and *Cymbeline* fleshing the skeleton out with every narrative and dramatic trick at Shakespeare's command, we are prepared to see *The Winter's Tale* modifying the genre in the direction of realism.[1]

The dramatic worlds of Sicilia and Bohemia, and the seas between, may seem more remote geographically than the ancient Britain of *Cymbeline*'s main plot and may seem, like *Pericles,* to participate temporally in the ancient Mediterranean cultures that appealed for aid and guidance to Olympian deities. But several factors help situate this play in the England of its early audiences: a court concerned with problems of succession, a rural sheep-shearing festival at which common English flowers are distributed (to characters bearing Greek names, of course), and the rogue Autolycus (named from Homer) flaunting the tricks of a petty offender of the Elizabethan underworld.[2] It relates further to the audience's world in the universal evocations of its ritualistic plot and by the richly ambiguous language that lends some verisimilitude to the psychological outlines of its characters.

We find many elements shared among the first three Romances beyond the generic similarities they exhibit.[3] *The Winter's Tale* shares with *Pericles* a structural break in the passage of many years between those dramatic events in which problems are established and those in which they are resolved. Both, in short, are clearly tragicomedies, hinged quite obviously in the middle.

But they differ in some of their structural effects. The linear and episodic plot of *Pericles* divides in two readily at Gower's prologue to act 4; similarly, *The Winter's Tale* can be divided in two, whether at the stage direction "Exit, pursued by a bear" that presages the last death in the story; at the old shepherd's words, "Now bless thyself: thou mett'st with things dying, I with things new-born"; or at the choral speech of Time that in position (the opening of act 4) parallels precisely Gower's overarching narrative in the earlier play. But the plot of *The Winter's Tale* is far less linear in effect than that of *Pericles*. As the action of the *Tale* moves from Sicilia to Bohemia and back to the Sicilia, the plot folds back upon itself in ways that can be compared either to the closing up of a diptych or to a cycle reverting in mythic and Neoplatonic fashion back to its beginning.[4]

The *Tale* shares with *Cymbeline* (and with *Othello*) the motif of furious jealousy in a husband convinced that his innocent wife is unfaithful. With *Pericles* and *Cymbeline* it shares the motif of a lost (or absent) daughter restored to her father as an agent in his transformation; an emphasis on magic; the theme of the otherwise good subordinate commanded to perform an evil action; doubling of characters; ritualistic effects; and, overwhelmingly, the sense of some transcendent power shaping the potentially or actually tragic elements into an overarching comic design. In *The Winter's Tale,* however, the help that providential power derives from a human agent takes on a new coloration in Paulina, who anticipates something found later in Prospero.

Date, Text, and Sources

The Winter's Tale was probably written in 1611, either concurrently with final touches on *Cymbeline* or soon after. Certainly the first recorded performance was at the Globe theater in May of that year, a month after a performance of *Cymbeline*. We have only the Folio text of 1623 for *The Winter's Tale*. When the plays were being performed frequently by the King's Men, there was no economic reason to print them for the public and many reasons to withhold them from rival companies. The text, a good one, seems to have been transcribed and then printed from Shakespeare's own working papers. Those places where the language is most garbled (as in act 1, scene 2, 137–46) work so well dramatically that there is no reason to blame obscurity on problems of transmission, as there so often is in the text of *Pericles*.[5]

The main source for *The Winter's Tale* is Robert Greene's prose romance *Pandosto,* published first around 1588—one of the many pieces of prose fiction that entertained members of Shakespeare's audiences when they were not in the theaters. Although he changed the names of most of the characters (Pandosto become Leontes; Bellaria, Hermione; Egistus, Polixenes; Fawnia, Perdita; and so on), Shakespeare followed so many of the details of Greene's text that the major changes he did choose to make are often worth noting. The most striking change was to transform a tragic narrative of jealousy, remorse, and divine retribution into a tragicomic drama with a self-proclaimedly happy ending. Greene's Queen Bellaria does actually die, along with her young son; after the lost daughter, Fawnia, returns to remind Pandosto of his injustice, the king kills himself. To know this is to take Leontes' guilt and repentance seriously, as Shakespeare surely did, but to see the restoration of happiness and order in the play (however qualified by the irreversible deaths of Mamillius and Antigonus) in a very positive light. This, the third of the Romances, would convince any contemporary, who would know his Greene the way we know the best-sellers or television series of recent decades, that Shakespeare was deliberately making new and happier patterns out of old and would set them to pondering the transformations.

The story of *The Winter's Tale* is not as complex as that of *Cymbeline*. Since complexity of language does so much to carry the plot forward, it will be interesting to compare the bare story with the closer analysis of the second scene that will open further discussions.

The Story

Act 1   Camillo and Archidamus, lords, respectively, of Sicilia and Bohemia, discuss the current visit of Polixenes, king of Bohemia, to the court of Leontes of Sicilia. They note the brotherly affection between the kings, forged in shared experiences in childhood. They indicate that Sicilia's hospitality is richer than that Bohemia will be able to offer in return when Leontes and his companions return the visit. In the second scene, Polixenes announces his departure after a visit of nine months, resisting repeated requests from Leontes that he stay. Leontes commands his queen, Hermione, to further his efforts. When her entreaties succeed, Leontes grows suspicious that he is being betrayed by guest and wife. He raves in innuendo to his son, Mamillius, and in direct accusation to a courtier, Camillo, who staunchly defends the queen's virtue. Leontes orders Camillo to poison Polixenes; instead Camillo warns him and flees with him to Bohemia.

Act 2   Hermione, tired in her late pregnancy, calls for her ladies to amuse Mamillius. The boy shows precocity and a sense of royal command in banter with them. His mother soon joins in the amusement. Leontes, his rage heightened by the flight of Polixenes and Camillo, enters, accuses Hermione directly of adultery, and, dismissing her gentle but firm denials, orders her to prison. His attendant lords, including Antigonus, protest. Leontes announces that to confirm his accusations he has sent messengers to the oracle at Delphi.

Paulina, Antigonus's wife, visits the prison where Hermione has just given birth to a daughter. Seeking to soften the king, Paulina takes the child into his presence. Raging—both at Paulina, the "mankind witch" who dares thus to confront him, and at the "bastard" he takes the child to be— Leontes first threatens to burn both mother and child and then orders Antigonus to expose the babe in "some remote and desert place quite out / Of our dominions."

Act 3   Leontes' messengers describe the sweet climate at Delphos and pray to Apollo to "turn all to the best."

At court, Leontes formally charges Hermione with infidelity. Denying the charge without hope that she will be believed, and ready to die, she calls on "powers divine" to defend her woman's honor—a "derivative from me to mine," her children. The messengers arrive with the oracle's defense of Hermione's chastity and its prediction that "the king shall live without an heir, if that which is lost be not found." Leontes rejects the message as untrue; immediately the news arrives that Mamillius has died. Leontes immediately sees this as Apollo's anger at his "injustice"; Hermione swoons and is carried offstage; Leontes plans reconciliation with those he has wronged; Paulina returns to report Hermione's death; Leontes vows prayers of repentance as his daily "recreation."

On a far shore in Bohemia, Antigonus has landed with the baby. In a dream, Hermione has asked that he call the child Perdita, she who has been lost, and has told him that he will never see his wife again. Setting the baby down, Antigonus "exit[s], pursued by a bear." An old shepherd and his son, a "clown," enter describing the death of Antigonus and the loss by storm of all mariners aboard the ship that carried him. They find the babe along with much gold and rejoice in their good fortune. Her name, Perdita, is conveyed in an attached note.

Act 4   Time, as chorus, spans the sixteen years that have passed between acts 3 and 4. Leontes has suffered overwhelming guilt, while far away Perdita has "grown in grace / Equal with wond'ring" at the comfortable rural home of her foster father, the old shepherd.

At the court of Bohemia, another scene of parting and remonstrance unfolds: Camillo tells Polixenes he has been summoned to Sicilia by the repentant Leontes but agrees to stay a little longer. They discuss rumors that the beautiful daughter of an affluent shepherd has engaged the affections of the young prince, Florizel.

Out on a footpath in Bohemia, the "rogue" Autolycus sings cheery, ribald songs. He meets the clown who has been sent to purchase supplies for the festival of sheep shearing and picks his pocket, allaying suspicion by complaining of having been robbed of his own fine clothes by a notorious rascal, "Autolycus." Mistress of the festivities at the sheep shearing, Perdita is wooed by Florizel, disguised as the gentle rustic, Doricles. Polixenes and Camillo, also disguised, are welcomed by Perdita. They prompt Florizel to confess that he is hiding his love for Perdita from his father. Polixenes unmasks and angrily forbids the match. Camillo suggests that Florizel and Perdita seek refuge in Sicilia with Leontes, who will assuredly welcome them. Autolycus, in the guise of a peddler, enters and sings more of his happy, ribald songs. He exchanges clothing with Florizel to aid the lovers' escape. Camillo muses that he will tell Polixenes of the flight to draw him to Sicilia and advance his own reconciliation with Leontes.

Act 5   In Sicilia, Cleomenes pleads with Leontes to forgive himself—his long years of penance have more than "paid down" his trespasses. Leontes, remembering Hermione with longing, cannot forget his guilt. While others ask him to marry again, Paulina continues to reproach him and exacts the promise that he will not marry without her leave. Florizel and Perdita enter, closely followed by the news that Polixenes is approaching. Florizel laments that Camillo has betrayed them. Touched by the lovers' fresh beauty and mutual love, Leontes resists Polixenes' letter asking that he arrest Florizel and promises to intercede for them.

Three gentlemen in conversation describe the scene of tearful wonder that ensued when Perdita's true identity was revealed by the old shepherd and clown who, through the action of Autolycus, had followed the lovers to Sicilia. The oracle has been fulfilled. Polixenes has forgiven Leontes and blessed the union of the prince and princess. The gentlemen tell also of Paulina's mixed emotions when the prevailing joy coincided with the confirmation of her husband's death. The shepherd and his son, now enriched by royal favor, encounter Autolycus, who thinks it prudent to promise to mend his ways.

The court assembles on Paulina's invitation to view a statue of Hermione, which, she says, she has had the noted Julio Romano execute for her.[6] Perdita kneels before the lifelike "lady" to implore a blessing. Paulina prolongs the marveling suspense, forbidding Perdita and Leontes to touch the work of art but offering to make the statue move. Before Hermione (for it is she) descends from her pedestal to harmonious music to embrace Leontes, Paulina protests that her "magic" is "lawful." Happy reunions ensue—wife with husband, mother with child. Hermione says her oracle-based hope of seeing Perdita again preserved her life. Paulina proposes now to withdraw to grieve for her own continuing loss; instead she is matched by command of the grateful Leontes with Camillo, "an honourable husband." Paulina leads them out, in order, to tell their several stories of events in "this wide gap of time."

The Slippery Language of Scene 2

As in life, so in this fiction, the necessity for each to tell a personal story in the hearing of others arises because the tales we tell ourselves of the events in which we participate rarely coincide with the way other participants understand the same events. One way of interpreting the fall that closed the gates of Eden to all children of Adam and Eve makes it a fall into alienation—not just from the God we cannot see again walking in the garden but also from the God we encounter in human relationship whenever we are truly united with others in love. Fallen human souls, enclosed in mortal bodies and bone-hard heads, enclosed in barriers of self, must work hard at interpreting words and events if the alienation that pushes us toward tragedy is to be overcome. But fallen human souls, and flawed minds, need help against the evil forces that prevail in the world of tragedy. The help offered by the deus ex machina in the first two Romances takes an interesting turn in this play—but that insight will be developed later.

Meanwhile, we see that the second long scene reflects "realistically" the inevitable problems raised by human language. The ease with which the lines between truth and falsity can blur is demonstrated here: as we participate imaginatively in the dramatic fiction we sense something of the dangers we all face in human communication. We sense also, through symbolic and mythic reverberations of the language, the outlines of the great changes in human life with which the play ultimately concerns itself.

When Polixenes announces his departure after "nine changes of the watery star," his phrase signifies to us openly the span of his absence from Bohemia, but as the scene unfolds we find, in retrospect, that the words can reinforce Leontes' suspicions; the visit has been just long enough to match the span of human gestation. The language readily transfers itself to notions of the inconstancy of woman. The interplay between an innocent phrase and the guilt it can bespeak to a suspicious ear typifies the opposition between innocence and sin that runs as motif throughout the scene.

While Hermione is urging their guest to stay, Leontes is ostensibly deep in private thought. But what he can overhear, in snatches and out of context, while Hermione and Polixenes talk lightly of the past will signify to him something very different from what is intended by the speakers.

Take Polixenes' memories, for instance: "We were . . . two lads that thought . . . to be boy eternal . . . twinn'd lambs that chang'd innocence for innocence" and "knew not the doctrine of ill-doing" (1.2.63–70). In his memory, the innocence of youth, the high idealism of the *puer aeternus,* is unqualified. Hermione's lighthearted response, "By this we gather / You have tripp'd since," does indicate awareness of the "doctrine of ill-doing" but no personal guilt on her part. This is the sort of social games playing her husband's rebuke for her silence has encouraged. Polixenes' rejoinder edges toward guilty ambiguity, especially to a listener already as prone to suspicion as Leontes:

> O my most sacred lady,
> Temptations have since then been born to's: for
> In those unfledg'd days was my wife a girl;
> Your precious self had not then cross'd the eyes
> Of my young playfellow.
>
>   (1.2.76–80)

The image of boy twins, exchanging innocence freely, darkens when temptation is equated to the female persons of the two wives. "Exchanging" becomes in this context explosive. The fuse is lit by Hermione's still "innocent" banter:

> Of this make no conclusion, lest you say
> Your queen and I are devils. Yet go on;
> Th'offences we have made you do we'll answer,
> If you first sinn'd with us, and . . .
>
>   . . . not
> With any but with us.
>
>   (1.2.81–86)

The plural pronouns lay the words wide open: as they blur the demarcations between two husbands and two wives it would be hard to prove that the syntax signifies parallels, not crossovers.

Few readers suspect Hermione as Leontes comes to do,[7] but few noticing these ambiguities would agree that Leontes' malignity is as totally unmotivated as that of Iago when he insinuates a similar malignity into the hitherto trusting soul of Othello. There is no doubt that the word structures lend themselves as readily to the dark interpretation Leontes comes to favor as to the truth and fidelity we as audience and readers locate in Hermione.

"A lady's Verily's / As potent as a lord's," Hermione protests when Polixenes says "verily" he "may not" stay. Here, too, playful language develops ambiguous reverberations. She who has just been addressed as "most sacred lady," a phrase that elevates her almost to the status of the Virgin Mary, is suggesting a relativity in truth that enables it to be claimed by opposing forces. With three repetitions of "verily" outweighing Polixenes' one, she prevails, but the victory is one of social grace, not of ultimate truth.

I turn now to the ambiguous word *grace*, which Hermione first uses in the sense I have just demonstrated. With "Grace to Boot!" (1.2.80) she applauds one of Polixenes' courtly compliments. She uses it playfully again to Leontes of an as yet undefined "good deed" she has done by speaking "to th' purpose," but when she finds that the deed was her acceptance of his offer of marriage, the tone deepens: "Tis Grace indeed."

It deepens, that is, when we see Hermione as the very model of chaste wifehood. But Leontes? He can trivialize it easily as Hermione goes on, lightly, to compare the occasions on which she "for ever earned a royal husband" and "for some while a friend." Shakespeare used that word, in a sense now obsolete, in *Measure for Measure:* "He hath got his friend with child" (1.4.29).[8]

Who is to interpret? The king, born and bred to earthly authority, never questions his own opinions—or his own lack of spousal trust—until the oracle, which he first rejects, seems confirmed by the death of a king to be, Mamillius. Royalty, proved mortal, seems also then as fallible as mortal.

Authority, Courtiership, and Sexual Hierarchy

Like the other Romances, and like any other fiction that focuses on a ruler as a major protagonist, *The Winter's Tale* explores the complex theme of authority. But unlike Antiochus, who is deliberately vicious, and unlike Cleon, Cymbeline, and at times Pericles, who are too passive (the first two hag-ridden, the third apathetic under the harsh power of lady Fortune), Leontes rules so vigorously as to be tyrannical, understanding his own actions as unquestionable and therefore right. In this one important dimension, the play represents Leontes' quest for a new understanding of himself as ruler, of others in the relationships they bear toward him, and of the place of ruler and ruled in a transformed system of values.

Since the dominant plot lines bear on relationships within the royal families of Sicilia and Bohemia, and most of those characters who are not royal are still defined by family structures (or, in the case of Autolycus, the lack thereof), the issue of authority in this play bears directly on sexual roles. The court becomes a large metaphor for the family in a patriarchal culture— hence my juxtaposition, in this section, of courtly and sexual politics.

Before moving on to the central family hierarchies in the plot, I consider a question that has arisen in the two earlier Romances: that of the quandaries that arise for courtiers whose rulers' decrees run counter to their own moral judgments. Of courtiers in this play, Camillo, Antigonus, and Paulina are most striking, but they have enough companions in quandary in Sicilia to support all the trust we are willing to invest in Hermione.

Camillo is first to be given a chance to remonstrate when Leontes turns his suspicions into open accusations against his queen. He sees the way the king is moving when asked, "How cam't, Camillo, / That he [Polixenes] did stay?" "At the good queen's entreaty" is one word longer than need be to an- swer the question, and "good" is one word too many for Leontes, who com- mands that it be dropped (1.2.219–22). As the accusations swell, so too do Camillo's defenses of his "most gracious mistress," his "most sovereign mis- tress," the "clouding" of whose name calls for his personal "vengeance." Camillo's words here, with his later diagnosis of the king's "truth" as "diseas'd opinion,"[9] demonstrate courage, fixed as Leontes is in his delusions, and powerful as he is to act upon his judgmental anger.

Camillo finally gives up open remonstrance with, "I must believe you, sir" (1.2.333): opposition to a "diseas'd" monarch must henceforth be covert. He accedes ostensibly to the king's command that he kill Polixenes, but one short soliloquy and one brief conversation hence, he and Polixenes are allied in their escape from Sicilia.

In the final two acts, Camillo demonstrates a similar resistance to the harsh commands of his new ruler, Polixenes, but not without mixed motivation. Helping Florizel and Perdita to escape to Sicilia may be less a matter of sup- port for the rebellious lovers than a stratagem to get his homesick self, with Polixenes, to Sicilia (4.4.662–67), where he knows a warm welcome from the repentant Leontes awaits them. For that to work, he must tell Polixenes of the lovers' flight. Before the happy outcome softens the impression of Camillo's duplicity, Florizel flatly calls it betrayal (5.1.192). We remember this instance of self-serving when the otherwise exemplary Camillo is matched by Leontes to Paulina. It qualifies her "happy" ending.

Antigonus and another "Lord," unnamed, defend Hermione against Leontes' "justice" when he sends her off to prison. The lord would lay down his life if Leontes would "accept . . . that the queen is spotless / I' th' eyes of heaven"; Antigonus, stirred to his masculine depths, would "by [his] honour" geld his three daughters if the queen "be honour-flaw'd" (2.1.130–47). The harsh illogicality of the threat cuts two ways. Primary is the sense that he knows such a horror would never be required of him since he trusts the queen absolutely. But a woman hearing him must flinch at a familiar consequence of masculine anger, that one "proved" instance of female misconduct will cast assumptions of guilt on all, and prompt reactions punitive for the innocent. We have already seen this instinctive masculine reaction demonstrated in Posthumus's misogyny when Iachimo has duped him.

Two scenes later, Antigonus's humane protectiveness extends to the newborn baby. To Leontes' challenge, "What will you adventure / To save this brat's life?" he responds "Anything, my lord . . . I'll pawn the little blood which I have left / To save the innocent." The language will be borne out by events, sadly, but the effect is not merely of foreshadowing. The laying down of a life for another (though the other be "innocent," not deemed guilty of that original sin "hereditary ours" [1.2.75]) has overtones the audience cannot miss. In starkest terms, we are driven to recognize that resistance to powerful evil in this world can call for total sacrifice.

Many male courtiers dare, for a time, to challenge Leontes, and, for a time, Leontes tolerates each. Paulina provokes a very different reaction when she enters to defend Hermione and intercede for the baby. "Away with that audacious lady!" the king thunders as soon as he sees Paulina enter. "Antigonus, / I charg'd thee that she should not come about me. / I knew she would." When Antigonus pleads himself helpless to keep his wife in line, he wryly rationalizes: "When she will take the rein I let her run." Paulina's opening speech belies her husband's insinuation that she is an unruly animal: "Good my liege, I come . . . your loyal servant, your physician, / Your most obedient servant . . . I say, I come / From your good queen."

Paulina's words are courageous—*physician* and *good* especially—but they are measured by courtesy. When the king mocks, "Good queen!" the courage swells: "I say good queen, and would by combat make her good, so were I / A man, the worst about you." Before she is eventually forced out, she hears herself called a "mankind witch . . . A most intelligencing bawd," a "crone," a "callat," a "gross hag! / And lozel." But no epithet stems the flow of words by which Paulina defends "the sacred honour of himself, his queen's / His hopeful son's, his babe's" against the king's own "slander" (2.3.61–129).[10] Paulina leaves only when subject to force: "I pray you, do not push me; I'll be gone." In the face of the verbal and physical abuse that a woman challenging masculine bastions of power must suffer,[11] Paulina exhibits a moral strength and tenacity more impressive than any other courtier's.

Her more important role in orchestrating the events that lead Leontes through remorse and repentance to reconciliation will be examined later. Meanwhile we turn to the scene of Hermione's trial (3.2).

A Woman's Verily

We have seen "A lady's Verily" prevail against Polixenes' intent to leave: in courtly games playing, "lords" will defer to "ladies." But what of those more desperate situations in which a woman's reputation and very life are at stake? Once her "lord," her master, has decided to count her "integrity . . . falsehood," it "shall . . . scarce boot [her] / To say 'not guilty'": he who holds the social and political power will determine how words will be receiv'd (3.2.25–27). In situations of such dead earnest, a woman's verily means very little.

Yet, like Paulina in her eloquent courage, Hermione must say what she can. She affirms her own dignity as "a great king's daughter, / The mother to a royal prince"—both claims, we note, dependent on her relationship to male power—and then staunchly accepts her peril: "For life, I prize it / As I weigh grief (which I would spare)." But for "honour, / 'Tis a derivative from me to mine, / And only that I stand for" (3.2.42–45). That "honour," a lady's, encompasses the correct social graces she has shown toward Polixenes—"such a kind of love as might become / A lady like me . . . even such . . . as yourself commanded." But more, her woman's "honour" rests on the assertion that the "love" she offered Polixenes was "So, and no other" (3.2.64–67). Her words in extremity prove predictably futile. To Leontes' further accusations she responds:

> Sir,
> You speak a language that I understand not:
> My life stands in the level of your dreams,
> Which I'll lay down.
> (3.2.79–82)

The silence of the metrical space after "Sir" is as eloquent as Hermione's acceptance of the nightmare that threatens her life and as the double-edged irony of Leontes' retort, "Your actions are my dreams."

Whose Actions? Whose Dreams?

Leontes simply intends the court to understand that Hermione's guilty actions occasion his nightmares. But the copula verb, whose function is to join two syntactical elements in a structure of equality or reciprocity, reflects the "dreams" back upon the "actions": the guilt he implies may have no more substance than the delusions of his deeply disturbed mind. Leontes' words expose the contests between falsity and truth, appearance and reality, "action" and "dream," even tragedy and comedy, that confront us in language, theater, and life. They prompt me to step back from practical interpretation to reflect briefly on what we have been doing.[12]

We are engaged in a complex process. As we interpret the dramatic actions unfolding for us in Shakespeare's language, we are doing in the theater of our minds what the characters within the fictions do in relation to each other. Between us and the characters, in any Shakespearean production, move the actors who must choose their tones of voice and their body language according to their—and their directors'—interpretation of Shakespeare's text. Beyond the theaters, and outside the rooms and libraries in which we work over the texts, spread other "texts": the history of Shakespeare's time, which links the family of King James to the plots of the Romances, and the history of our own time, which predisposes us to see the dangers of unquestioned power and control, whether in mushroom clouds, ecological disasters, domestic injuries—or dramatic texts.

We, interpreting texts, reconstruct them in the personal theaters of our minds and the texts we write and read. In Aristotle's phrase, interpreters imitate actions as truly as the playwright does. But the critical mimeses in which we are engaged do not merely reflect the literature we read or the "real" lives we live. In the webs of language in which we all participate, the process of imitation, of re-presentation, works to make present that which can never be wholly or unambiguously present. The process unfolds inconclusively—cutting through barriers that divide levels of interpretation from each other and those that divide skull-locked men and women from each other. Insofar as we participate with vigorous inquiry in the fictions, we change our capacities to participate with vigorous inquiry in the "real" lives of those who share our personal histories—to understand a little, to interpret with the judgment that, arising from empathy, leads to conclusions more equitable than those of unquestioning, autocratic judgment.

My argument will never prove—nor is it trying to prove—that Shakespeare understood his own linguistic-dramatic efforts in precisely this way. If it refreshes and expands our awareness as readers, it serves its primary purpose. If, further, it convinces us that art does interconnect, mysteriously and intricately, with life, that the interconnections go far beyond the resemblances of a reflection in a mirror to the object reflected, it participates in

Shakespeare's lifelong preoccupation with art's bridging of the gap between illusion and reality.[13]

In *The Winter's Tale* the most striking moment of this bridging comes when Hermione, presented by Paulina as a statue, a work of art, steps down and presents herself in embrace to her husband—not a statue, not an impossible dream projected by the residual *puer* or youth in her ostensibly adult husband, but a warm and breathing woman. The art of Paulina has worked to transform Leontes' false image of perfection into his realization of an absence that calls for fulfillment not by an artifact of the imagination but by a person.

Now we move on to consider yet again the illusory world projected by a man who is possessed by the archetype of the *puer* aeternus and the problems real women have when subjected to his *dreams*.

The *Puer*, the *Senex*, and Honor

Thus far, when speaking of the *puer aeternus*, I have followed the insights that Marie-Louise von Franz developed from Jung's own usages of the term. We have seen that the *puer* is obsessed with the image of purity in woman, an obsession justified in his inner world by the high ideals he holds before him on life's quest and by the accordingly high image he holds of his own role. The obsession is rooted in infancy. What the "boy eternal" (1.2.65) is seeking is the perfect maternal figure (or at times the parental-paternal, since the nurturing unity can include a man), lost when the *puer* first began to realize that his wish was no guarantee of its own fulfillment.[14] Since life unfolds on a chronological continuum, experiences of infancy color youth, maturity, and age.

Several post-Jungian analysts, chief among them James Hillman, have followed an ancient and medieval convention in associating the archetype of the *puer* with that of the *senex* or old man.[15] Their insights are instructive for Leontes, Polixenes, and Prospero and for the Pericles of the last two acts of his play. Surprisingly, they bear also on the figure of Autolycus and, as we shall see in the next chapter, on Ariel and Caliban.

The positive *puer*, we have seen, is a questing idealist, always on the move, like Pericles perambulating the Mediterranean world, searching, among other perfections, for the perfect woman. A youth driven by this archetype may marry, but his understanding of his relationship with his wife will be so narcissistic that he will see her primarily as a reflection of his own perfection. (Thinking back to the narcissism of both Posthumus and Imogen early in their story, we recognize that both males and females can be propelled by *puer* consciousness.) If the union with a female brings forth the recognition and assimilation of the anima archetype, the *puer* comes down to mother earth and progresses toward the enlarged selfhood Jung speaks of as the goal of individuation. He will be driven thereafter neither by the *puer* figure nor by its polar opposite, the *senex,* but will be able to draw on the positive elements this double archetype represents, incorporating them with elements from other archetypes into a well-rounded psyche.

But *puer* consciousness does not always progress along a positive path. The *puer,* representative of and drawn to the transcendentally spiritual, "is weak on earth because it is not at home on earth." It is impatient, vulnerable, and, although changeable, it resists development. "When it must rest or withdraw from the scene, then it seems to be stuck in a timeless state . . . out of tune with time."[16] Hillman's insights seem tailored to fit the "wide gap of time" during which Leontes endlessly repeated his rituals of repentance and go some way toward explaining the otherwise inexplicable dallying of Pericles, who waits until his daughter is full grown before seeking to reclaim her.

If the *puer* on his quest toward selfhood loses his spiritual purpose and strays "through the halls of power towards the heart-hardened sick old king," that negative *senex* prevents the internal development of the archetype of the wise old man—the positive *senex.* The chronological age of the aging *puer* is relatively unimportant; critics have estimated that the rigid, irascible Leontes of the early acts is about twenty-eight. But the *puer*-driven man who does not come to know the anima within, his internal principle of love, life, inspiration, will come under the sway of the *senex* years before his time. If only he could keep the dynamism and idealism of youth and assimilate them to the positive attributes of age—order, responsibility, and wisdom! When the two poles of the *puer-senex* archetype are both in play, all is well. But the person driven by one with the other repressed—the *puer* only or the *senex* only—becomes trouble personified, for self and others.

The negative *senex,* flipping into power when the *puer* goes underground, has a number of attributes instructive for readers of the Romances: tendencies to melancholy and depression (the counterparts to the *puer*'s abstractions from the real world); a "hardening of consciousness"[17] that produces egocentricity, rigidity, irascibility, cold judgmentalism. Some or all of these traits are recognizable in Pericles (depression), Cymbeline (irascibility), Leontes (irascibility and judgmentalism), and even in that more positive wise old man, Prospero (irascibility).

Now to Leontes, Polixenes, and Florizel. The *puer,* idealist that he is, always means well. If he is born and bred to rule, he will be conditioned to see himself as perfect judge, defining his own understanding of any complex matter as the truth and acting accordingly with unquestioning authority. The description defines Leontes, but it can be extended to define young men (like Posthumus) who are kings only metaphorically as rulers within a love relationship or marriage. Since the kingdoms of *The Winter's Tale* should be read primarily as metaphors for the more universal structures of family and friendship, we often need to interpret Leontes' actions more as those of an authoritarian husband, a *puer* turned *senex*, than as those of a king.

As *puer-senex*, Leontes encounters universal problems. Having married a woman as royal as himself, projecting on her the image of the Virgin who blends eternal strength and unspotted purity with the maternal solicitude of the queen of heaven, he sees her undergoing the domestic changes the "watery" moon ordains for woman—the fatigues of pregnancy, the "spot of childbed taint,"[18] and, probably worse, the diversion of her attention from him by duties to her offspring. When his "virgin" becomes so palpably human, so changed—and perfection is not expected to change—deep and undefined anxieties come to the surface, ready to fasten on any plausible pretext.

Leontes' reactions to Hermione and Polixenes in the second scene are not mad in the sense of motiveless malignity; they are mad in the sense that they push to an absolute extreme, to absurdity, the self-confident "logic" that the *puer* turned *senex* substitutes for his undefined and misinterpreted anxieties. Leontes projects the frailties of the inner self he still idealizes onto the objectified scapegoats he makes of his wife and boyhood friend. The anxieties arising from "betrayal" by a mother are translated into anxieties about "betrayal" by the two figures who have formed Leontes' current circle of affection.

Polixenes is in some senses a double for Leontes. When Camillo tells their stories using third-person plural pronouns (1.1.21–32), and Polixenes extends and confirms the effect by using the first-person plural (1.2.62–75), the same verbs serve for both. As double, Polixenes is experienced by Leontes as uncanny—he reminds Leontes of oedipal and homoerotic impulses that get in the way of his loving a wife.[19] There is, then, an additional impulse to anxiety welling up in Leontes. Seeing the two he has loved best since he outgrew infancy in affectionate conversation with each other, Leontes is tossed back into an infant's turmoil, feeling outpowered (he has failed where another now succeeds), abandoned, betrayed. To understand him in this way is not to make light of a *senex*'s tyrannical injustice. But temper tantrums are more forgivable in a child than in a man. If we can forgive the child in

Leontes, we will accept, a little more readily, the moment when Hermione steps silently back into his arms.

The self-absorption of the child becomes, in the adult male under the influence of the *senex,* a preoccupation with personal honor. Since this is a tale of love, not war, Leontes is no Hotspur. His honor is vested in his image of himself as unquestioned authority over the unspotted kingdom to which Hermione belongs. When, tormented by insecurity, he looks outward for a cause and projects one on his wife and his friend, his deepest wound, we see, is to the honor he equates to his very life:

> Go play, boy, play: the mother plays. and I
> Play too; but so disgrac'd a part, whose issue
> Will hiss me to my grave: contempt and clamour
> Will be my knell.
>
> (1.2.187–90)

Hermione has been conditioned to share the patriarchal attitudes of Leontes: her long-suffering sweetness in the face of manifest injustice, like that of patient Griselda, follows the model of feminine strength held up to womanhood in any society dominated by masculine values.[20] She spiritedly defends her honor at her trial (humbly and subserviently in terms of reliance on the gods for vindication). She declares she does so on behalf of her family. Her own life, so painful now, she will gladly sacrifice, as a good woman should: "Sir, spare your threats: / The bug which you would fright me with, I seek . . . The crown and comfort of my life, your favour, / I give for lost" (3.2.91–95).

Once the action moves to Bohemia, rural and pastoral settings and characters soften the patriarchal and courtly values represented by Camillo and Polixenes, the latter at least representative of a *senex* when he acts the authoritarian father. At the sheep-shearing festival, Perdita, lamenting Florizel's humble disguise as Doricles worries how the king would "look, to see his work, so noble, / Vilely bound up." Florizel refers his humble disguise to the stories of "the gods themselves" who "humbling their deities to love, have taken / The shapes of beasts" to visit mortal maidens, or (like Apollo) of a "poor humble swain / As I seem now." Then he redefines honor in a way quite alien to men who define it in terms of possession and reputation:

> Their transformations
> Were never for a piece of beauty rarer,
> Nor in a way so chaste, since my desires

Run not before my honour, nor my lusts
Burn hotter than my faith.
(4.4.31–35)

The syntax is ambiguous. The word *chaste* refers first to Perdita, the "piece of beauty," but it then attaches itself forward to Florizel's "honour" and the "faith" that balances the urgency of his "lusts." The ambiguity reveals that, for Florizel, self and beloved form a unity and harmony that encompasses both the flames of sexual desire and the chaste "honour" of those who restrain desire until it can be lawfully expressed. Through the love that has grown out of his desire for the forthright maiden he believes to be no more than a shepherdess, Florizel—a generation younger than Leontes—has reached a maturity Leontes has yet to know.

This redefines honor in terms neither of masculine possession nor of feminine asexuality. Although Perdita's behavior is totally chaste, her ardor is never in doubt from the moment she appears as a figure of "Flora," a goddess who represents sexuality in most of her Renaissance manifestations. The ardor suffuses her address to Florizel at 4.4.130–32. Such a redefinition belongs to the fictive world of pastoral. Hierarchical and patriarchal societies, represented by the court, always assign the honors of war and possession (not very different from each other in feminist thinking) to men and the honor of sexual purity to women. Their highest genres are epic and tragedy. Pastoral, on the other hand, builds on the (in the male-defined genres, lower) values of retreat, receptivity, and sexual generation. Although I question any assumption that the optimism of *The Winter's Tale* is absolute, I find some indication of trust in the possibility of transformation in social attitudes in this representation of Florizel's advance over *puer-senex* thinking on "honour."

Before proceeding to Florizel's Perdita as a richer representation of the virgin archetype than Hermione, I want to look at the strange rascal Autolycus, who, negating all forms of honor, nobility, and humane concern, nonetheless inhabits the happier acts of this play.

The Role of Autolycus

What is Autolycus, named for the thieving son of Mercury and ancestor to the wily Ulysses, doing here in the pastoral world of love, with the noble Perdita and Florizel, with the trustworthy old shepherd and his honest but clownish son? What is he doing in Sicilia, the place of refuge and the birth of reconciliation?

Literal answers are easy enough to offer. Autolycus is singing dirty songs, playing confidence games at the expense of the unwary, peddling ribbons and other trifles to tempt an innocent eye, delivering in the end an absurd promise to reform. His antics entertain Shakespeare's audiences, just as within the fiction he entertains the decent rustics at the festival of the wool harvest. He serves the plot directly twice: he shifts clothing with Florizel, enabling him to escape a father's wrath with his beloved, and he directs the old shepherd and his son to Sicilia where they are able to reveal Perdita's true identity. The latter incident holds the clues to the deeper significance we sense but must struggle to define. This son of Mercury is as hard to pin down as his mercurial father, but he calls us to fathom his meaning: Mercury-Hermes is guide of souls and father of hermeneusis or interpretation.[21]

In asides, Autolycus confesses that "though I am not naturally honest, I am sometimes so by chance" (4.4.712–13) and that the good he has done to shepherd and clown has been "against his will" (5.2.124–5). His envy at "the blossoms of their fortune" prompts the second aside and undercuts the credibility of his promise that he will seriously mend his ways. After all, any hope of further gain from this fortunate pair will depend on the trust the rascal hopes to promote by his promise of transformation.

His very presence, untrustworthy as he continues to be, helps bridge the boundaries between fictive art and life. This story in which all seems to come together happily is not set in a true Eden, we see, but in a world realistically harboring a devil, calling yet for vigilant interpretation of others' language. This said, its converse also emerges: a world where the power of evil is represented by an entertaining rascal whose actions turn to good, whatever his motivation, is one we need not fear too seriously. The greater evil of a tyrannous king has been transmuted, in part through the actions of the rascal.

The shift of clothing by which Autolycus enables Florizel to escape is superficially simple to understand. Autolycus enjoys the advantage, clearly, of trading a peddler's rags for the relative riches of the prince's rural but festive guise. But a shift of clothing in Shakespeare is always worth pondering. As Cloten was tied in uncanny ways by clothing to Posthumus, so here we sense some mystery. Hillman, a mercurial writer on the mercurial aspects of the *puer,* once more can be our guide.

"When we stand in the image [of the trickster and soul guide] and view hermetically, the problem of black and white becomes irrelevant . . . Hermes son Autolykos . . . changes them back and forth opportunistically in accordance with the situation." The linkage between Autolycus and Florizel need not signify evil in the latter: garment shifts are not doctrine and do not require moralizing. What we do see is that as the *puer* moves toward selfhood (and Florizel is boyish and idealistic, even though we find he does not share the *puer*'s dehumanizing projection of self onto a virgin figure), he will meet situations in which good and evil are inextricably mixed. Sons owe allegiance to fathers; lovers owe allegiance to each other. Situations that in tragedy will tear an Antigone or an Othello apart can have different issue in the story of a clever youth. Florizel turns trickster to escape and buy time without incurring any but a *senex*'s adverse judgment. "Puer opportunism is . . . an instinctual adaptation to psychic realities," a stage in growth toward the fuller psychic being that can contend with worldly evils without disaster.[22]

The Female Principle: Mamillius, Hermione, and Perdita

Let us start this discussion with names, first with the name of the young prince, son to Hermione and brother to Perdita, whose death is the darkest of the irreversible evils in this tragicomedy. "Mamillius" is Shakespeare's name: the parallel character in *Pandosto* is Garinter. For a prince whose character is extolled as the epitome of youthful masculinity, the name is strange. Only its suffix sounds masculine; the first two syllables link it to a group of words denoting the female nipple or breast.[23] Mamillius's name works against the interpretation of his fatal illness that Leontes proposes: "To see his nobleness, / Conceiving the dishonor of his mother! / He straight declin'd . . . and fix'd the shame on't in himself." Mamillius is no young Hamlet, sickened by female sexuality. Were he so, his very name would have been the death of him long before he is forced to observe his father's cruelty and injustice toward his mother. He has accorded her a playful affection in their brief conversation together (2.1.21–32) and, earlier, a bemused defense against his father's raving accusations (1.2.208).

The death of Mamillius signifies more than the victimization of innocence under evil,[24] although the death of the son of a king often means that, in myth and scripture as in history. It signifies also the death in Leontes' Sicilia of those softer and nourishing virtues that are often regarded as feminine, although males too may be marked by "the milk of human kindness," to their detriment in a world that values power more than love.[25]

Although the particular child's death is irreversible, what he represents thematically is restored to Sicilia in Florizel. Leontes doubly regains a son in this son of his double, this husband to his daughter. Florizel's name, even more than that of Mamillius, suggests the union of male and female: "zell" is an archaic form of zeal, ardent love, and "Flora," goddess of the springing flowers, is the love name he himself gives Perdita, the "queen of curds and cream" (4.4.2, 161).

Hermione's name rarely attracts attention: Shakespeare's queen is so much more memorable than the classical character for whom she is named that "Hermione" now signifies to most a chaste and long-suffering wife whose closest sisters in literary typology are Desdemona and Chaucer's Griselda.

The Greek compound means "pillar-queen."[26] For the "herm" syllable, a glance at a Greek lexicon adds to "pillar" the suggestions of "prop," "rock," "bedpost." "Herm" as an English word signifies a pillar-supported statue of a male head, often used in ancient times as a boundary marker.[27] All of these variants open possibilities as we consider Hermione's role. She is certainly treated by Leontes like a bedroom thing, a "bedpost"; her integrity and passive strength under assault are "rock" hard; and Leontes' encouragement of her conversation with Polixenes, taken with his possessiveness, puts the unfortunate queen out on an exposed boundary. As a prop she supports the rigid male head that represents, in its turn, the *senex* who sees his spouse in utterly conventional and servile terms. When Leontes' perspective of Hermione as directly under him, supporting only him, is shaken by her friendly banter with his double (and unconscious rival) Polixenes and by the advanced pregnancy that will divert her support to a life newer and more fragile, the *senex* loses his balance and his head.

Etymology may be enough in itself to account for Shakespeare's name for the queen who in *Pandosto* is called Bellaria. But when we look at the sad tales of the ancient Hermione, evocative patterns emerge. Homer's Hermione was the daughter of Helen and Menelaus, abandoned by Helen when Paris carried her off to Troy. Thus Hermione's name was closely associated with an adultery of which she herself was innocent. Homer's Hermione endured the threat of an unjust death and marriage to a violent man, Orestes, who, when tried for the murder of his mother, escaped penalty. Orestes was defended by Apollo's denial that a mother is in any sense more important "than the inert furrow in which the husbandman casts his seed" and by the deciding vote of that most masculine of female Olympians, Athena-Diana.[28]

The analogies need not be labored. Shakespeare's Hermione is witty, intelligent, and chaste, but in pregnancy clearly touched by sexuality. She is so strong in adversity that women as well as men cannot fail to admire her. But this strong good woman's forbearance—with her willingness to embrace the husband who has grievously wronged her, caused the death of her firstborn, and exposed her second born—reflects a masculine dream of femininity, not the self-sufficiency of the pagan virgin archetype we see more clearly in Perdita than in her mother.

The one moment of the play that works best to justify the problematic embrace of reconciliation is that in which Leontes tells Paulina that the "dear stone" is much more "wrinkled" and "aged" than the beautiful wife he remembers. "Because eternity is changeless, that which is governed only by the puer does not age," Hillman notes. But Leontes, face to face with the changes of many watery moons and years, accepts the imperfections with no diminishment of his longing for the wife who would, living, look like this. The *puer-senex* powers that have been fueling his actions drop away in his recognition of longing for a specific, time-flawed, woman. The moment is like that in which Pericles confronts his memories of Thaisa in her name. Not the projected dream and adjunct but the particular woman draws the husband's love. Hermione, hearing all this as (true to her name) she stands motionless on her pedestal, may find in it the justification she needs for belief in Leontes' transformation.

Perdita's name—"the lost one" in the female inflection—is man given in several senses. Leontes has imposed on her innocence the exposure that "loses" her to Sicilia[29]; Antigonus has attached the name to her swaddling clothes; and the fostering shepherd has used it in her upbringing. Her name—chosen by the mother who knows male power all too well—suits all too well any girl-child born into a patriarchy ruled by the *puer-senex* polarity. Though her name is tied to her victimization as infant, Perdita represents also, like Mamillius, the loss to the court of Sicilia of those gentle, loving, and relating motives in the psyche that are symbolically feminine.

In pastoral Bohemia, Perdita wears her name proudly, and more honestly and independently than most men wear theirs. At her festival, the men from the court are disguised by name as well as attire; Autolycus is also disguised; and even the old shepherd and his son wear a social dignity that comes from the gold Antigonus left with the abandoned child, a dignity in this sense not their own. But Perdita is Perdita,[30] in her own mind no more or less than she seems—beautiful and witty by nature, modestly well dressed by good fortune, warm and commanding as mistress of the feast, ardently in love but fully concerned lest her noble lover fall into trouble because of her modest circumstances.

Perdita is in the most obvious sense a virgin—fully virtuous, innocent of sexual trespass though not of sexual desire. But her purity is not that of a votaress of Diana: it is neither tantalizingly unreceptive to male approach nor secluded from it as Thaisa and Hermione are when sequestered from their husbands. This forthrightly nubile girl is defined by her amatory relationship to Florizel and by her daughterly relationship to the old shepherd, Leontes, and Polixenes. She lives on the very boundary between daughterhood and wifehood, in both instances in close relationship to the masculine principle. All the more remarkable then is the decisive intelligence and moral aplomb in her dialogues with both Florizel and Polixenes, lover and future father-in-law, respectively.[31] These mark her as virginal in the most ancient sense of all, the self-sufficiency in the face of masculine strength that links her back to Marina.

But unlike Marina's, Perdita's female strength grows with her love. We have already noted her concern that her lover may fall under his father's censure for his masquerade in the festive dress that Autolycus will find such an improvement over his peddler's rags (4.4.18–22). She also feels abashed at the very thought that the king might surprise her in her "borrowed flaunts," a festive finery above her station; although she straightforwardly accepts her current status in the social hierarchy, she knows that discovery will threaten "this purpose" of their love and may do so with special force if her garments seem presumptuous. But on stage she and "Doricles" are matched in the costumes that are for her above, for him below, the proper social station. Their moral equality, thus emblematically established, is reinforced by Florizel's words: "Or I'll be thine, my fair, / Or not my father's. For I cannot be / Mine own, nor anything to any, if / I be not thine" (4.4.42–45). Strengthened in her own self-assertiveness by Florizel's declaration of his selfhood in the mutuality of love, Perdita can match Polixenes gracefully in the ironic debate on the breeding of flowers. Within the fiction, she does not know who this aristocrat may be, but she stands her ground against him on matters of both intellect and morality. The audience, knowing her identity, sees her vindicated yet again as fit consort to a prince.

The debate starts with the simple social gesture of a gift of flowers from the mistress of the feast to two newcomers and embraces as it unfolds many of the major themes of the Romances, and of romance as genre. Perdita dismisses, from her offerings, "carnations and streak'd gillyvors, / Which some call nature's bastards," propagated by grafting, "an art which, in their piedness, shares / With great creating nature." She prefers natural over artistic creation as befits the pastoral occasion and her own rural nurture. But Polixenes counters with a conventional argument based in Neoplatonic philosophy: since all creation flows down through the various strata of the cosmos from the One source, "nature is made better by no mean / But nature makes that mean." "Over that art, which you say adds to nature, is an art / That nature makes." Polixenes goes on to praise the husbandman's art that "marr[ies] / A gentle scion to the wildest stock" to "make conceive a . . .

baser kind / By bud of nobler race." Such art, mending nature, "itself is nature."

Perdita gracefully concedes his principle (which Polixenes fails to recognize as applicable to the marriage he will soon oppose, thinking the girl's nature and nurture both deficient) but she still refuses to have anything to do with the flowers of bastardizing art. "No more than, were I painted, I would wish / This youth should say 'twere well, and only therefore / Desire to breed by me." Her final sally, whether she guesses her antagonist's identity or not, affirms her natural worth against all that "artful" nurture might have done to improve her. It also shows a virginal vigor insisting, not shrewishly, on the last word and the loving fervor from which she draws her strength.

That commonplace of Renaissance pastoral, the nature-nurture debate, introduced here pointedly and enigmatically, will arise again in *The Tempest*. But we turn now from it to matters related to the larger questions of nature and art raised by Paulina's "magic."

Paulina: No Deus ex Machina, "Mankind witch"

We have seen Paulina's courage in the face of tyranny provoking a misogynistic tirade from Leontes, embedded in which was the epithet "mankind witch." The phrase labeled her by two major and conventionally related offenses, sexual perversity and the practice of forbidden arts. In a rigid patriarchy, any female strength that contradicts the imposed norms of unthreatening femininity automatically provokes such taunts. A woman is held to be no woman if she fails to conform to the masculine dream.[32] Moreover, she will be suspected of links to devilish powers to support her usurping strength. History demonstrates that independent women, acting out of strength and wisdom in the cause of good,[33] have been frequently persecuted as witches for the knowledge and behavior that is seen as far less dangerous in a man like Prospero.

Mamillius's death, confirming the oracle's support for Paulina's position, alters Leontes' responses. Self-accused, he welcomes the power of this strong woman to punish his tyranny. Her very name suggests the epistles of Paul, which define and condemn human sin in the context of a hope for redemption that hinges on repentance. I warn again that explicit doctrine need not be preached, by Shakespeare or any reader, for us to hear reverberations in Paulina's name that link her to a male model of unquestionable authority. Those who find such reverberations powerful will find in the "resurrection" and the gracious forgiveness offered by Paulina's mistress a representation, however incomplete, of Paul's lord and master. In Hermione, Paulina serves not the devil, lord of witches, but a human channel of divine love. As we shall see, though, that human channel offers links to more than one divine myth.

In the final scene, years after the accuser's anger has cooled, Paulina recalls the charge of witchcraft when she declares that the "spell" by which she brings Hermione to life "is lawful." We know, of course, that the "art" that enables the statue to move into Leontes' arms is that of "great creating nature," the art of God sustaining Hermione through the trials that have deepened the marks of time in her face.

Hermione utters no words to Leontes in their embrace or to Camillo, who challenges her to prove she lives by speaking. Only when Paulina leads Perdita to seek a blessing does the mother finally speak: "You gods look down, / And from your sacred vials pour your graces / Upon my daughter's head!" Her maternal love, sustained by the hope the oracle gave, has "preserv'd" her "to see the issue." Hermione's last word in the play can be paraphrased as "outcome," but to do so impoverishes its meaning. This play is about the saving grace of the Nature the Renaissance philosophers saw in the earthly Venus, the medieval philosophers deified as *Natura Naturans,* and the ancients celebrated in the mother-daughter mysteries of Demeter and Persephone. In the upturn of Nature's annual cycle, figured as transparently in the reunion of Hermione with Perdita as in the older myths, a "sad tale" yields to merry spring, and all the happy tales the persons of the play will tell each other after "good Paulina / Lead[s them] hence." In this final ritualistic scene, three women—maiden, mother, and crone—dominate, three avatars of the ancients' triple goddess. Through her, the great creating Nature, the love that issues from nature redresses wrongs and restores social and spiritual balance.

One wry observation demands concluding space. Only after all has been ceremoniously resolved under Paulina's apparent control do we realize that Leontes, again in command, is denying her wish to escape the happiness she cannot share. Without a word of courtship or permission, he is matching her to Camillo and telling her what she must direct others to do. For a male playwright, a happy ending sees all power reinvested in those to whom it traditionally has belonged. Paulina's manifest power must be governed by another husband—however ineffectual in this sense Antigonus once proved to be.

Chapter Five

"Your tale, sir, would cure deafness": *The Tempest*

Unlike the first two Romances but like *The Winter's Tale, The Tempest* is not named for a protagonist. Yet one character, Prospero—erstwhile duke, father of a marvelous virgin-daughter, magician in command of airy spirits, slave master to an earthy monster—dominates the play from the moment we learn that his "art" has raised the tempest until the moment his voice falls silent after the epilogue. In this play we participate in many transformations, but the greatest of all is Prospero's.

Everything happens along lines radiating from Prospero's center to the sea circumference of his island. Even the antics of Caliban and the drunken clowns undergird all else, since Caliban himself comes to represent to Prospero, and to us—among other things—a grotesque avatar of the old man.

The themes of generation and regeneration so prominent in the previous Romances are still important in *The Tempest,* but the tightness of this play's structure,[1] with its commanding triad of Ariel (spirit), Prospero (will or controlling agent), and Caliban (body), contributes to the impression that the action represents, above all, something going on in Prospero's own psyche, something of great moment for us all. Like him, we are individuals, born into families and shaped by positive or negative relationships with the members of our families. (If solitaries like Autolycus and Jaques, we are defined by the negative space that replaces family for us, as for them.) Like Prospero, we find that the selves defined by a family dynamic operate characteristically in larger interpersonal spheres. And like him—"that's my brave spirit"; "this thing of darkness I acknowledge mine"—we can sense in introspection a whole cast of personae occupying by turns the center we normally encompass in the word *self.* Centripetally, "self"-control, and centrifugally, control of others by the "self," are the major interlinked themes of Prospero's play—and both relate to the symbolic vehicle of control, Prospero's magic. Since Prospero's "self" in the fiction can be taken to represent many functions, certain subthemes in addition to magic—political authority, gender hierarchy, bondage and freedom, language—figure in his story. In comparison to that of Florizel and Perdita, the story of young love between Ferdinand and Miranda seems almost a digression in this play, although it is necessary to the completion of Prospero's scheme, and his own transformation. Primarily, then, I read this play as the representation of one man, and I find him self-locked at the *senex* pole of the *puer-senex* archetype until the power of his own alchemical magic takes its salutary effect on him. He who baptizes others in the tempest-tossed sea is at last baptized into new awareness through the alchemical magic of his own art.

Until that time of resolution this tightly structured drama remains divided. On its surface, in its main plot, we see the controlled calm that is first asserted in the second scene; underneath, in the grotesque subplot, we sense that the antics of Caliban and his drunken fellows represent a personal turbulence in Prospero merely masked by his ostensible control. The theme suggested by the title of *The Tempest* pervades the whole of the play, not just the opening scene to which I turn after the next two sections of this chapter.

Date, Text, and Sources

Like *The Winter's Tale* and *Cymbeline*, *The Tempest* was first published in the Folio of 1623, there given pride of place as first in the volume. Reliable evidence places an early production, if not the first, at court in the fall of 1611. Because of its elaborate stage directions, some editors think the Folio text was set from a good transcript of the prompt-copy used in an actual production. Such elaborate directions might alternatively, or further, be explained by the influence of similar instructions in the scripts for the masques popular in court circles at the same time or by the hypothesis that Shakespeare had himself retired to Stratford before the actual production of the play. Whatever the reason or reasons, the stage directions add strong and positive dimensions to the experience of reading the play and influence many of the decisions taken in mounting any production.

The most important "sources" for this highly original play are less sources than catalysts: the "Bermuda Pamphlets" and other texts reporting travels and discoveries in the New World.[2] Certainly a play beginning with a shipwreck on an island inhabited by a "Caliban" whose name and nature recall the "cannibals" of such reports owes something to current interest in the strange New World. But the changes Shakespeare makes, which include locating his island in the Old World of the Mediterranean instead of the Caribbean, suggest that the historical topicality of this play is more apparent than real. *The Tempest* does, however, share with the travel literature, and with Montaigne's essay "On Cannibals" that the same voyagers' tales had prompted, a deep interest in the nature-nurture debates raised repeatedly in the Renaissance pastorals that stem from Hellenistic Greek fiction. Of these, only the Montaigne essay (in the contemporary translation by Florio) can be taken as an undisputed source, and that for only very small portions of the play.

Other intertexts that have been proposed as sources include *The Aeneid*, the tales of voyages in medieval saints' legends, and texts in alchemy, magic, and daemonology, both ancient and current.[3] It is probable that Aristotle's discussion of the unities of time, place, and action in the *Poetics* (just coming into prominence in English poetic theory at this time) influenced the tight narrative structure of *The Tempest*, so atypical of romance as a genre and of the other Romances. But when all is said, *The Tempest* remains one of the most original of Shakespeare's dramatic structures. Everything that contributes to it is transmuted, almost alchemically, in the tight integrity of its text.

The Story

Act 1   The play opens on a scene of mounting chaos: on the deck of a storm-tossed ship mariners battle the elements, impeded alike by well-meaning and derisive members of the courtly group who are returning from Tunis to Italy after the wedding of the king of Naples's daughter. The ship is breaking apart as some aboard work, some scoff, and some pray.

Quiet prevails as the scene shifts to Prospero and Miranda, "before Prospero's cell" on the "uninhabited island" announced as setting at the head of the page naming "the Actors." The magician-father assures his sympathetically fearful daughter that although his "Art" has indeed raised the storm, he has calmed it without hurting any of those whose lives have appeared threatened. Shedding his magic mantle, he tells his daughter the story he has withheld from her during the twelve years of their habitation on the island.

Once the scholarly duke of Milan, Prospero lost his dukedom when his concentration on his "secret studies" opened the opportunity for his evil brother, Antonio—with the aid of Alonso, king of Naples—to oust him and take power for himself. With his tiny daughter Prospero was set adrift in a leaky boat, which, with the help of providence, he says, carried them to this desert island. A good courtier, Gonzalo, had secretly stocked the boat with food, Prospero's clothing, and precious library. Now "Fortune" has brought his "enemies" to this shore. Putting Miranda to sleep, Prospero summons his spirit, Ariel. Gleefully they delight in the furor they have raised, but Prospero does demand assurances that no one has been hurt. The victims of the storm are not only safe, says Ariel, but after their immersion in the sea are "fresher than before." Ariel asks to be rewarded by the liberty Prospero has promised, but Prospero testily reminds him he still owes some debt for having been released from the evil spell of "the foul witch, Sycorax," who had bound him in "a cloven pine," to leave the island to her son, the "freckled whelp" Caliban. Ariel departs with the promise of liberty in due course.

Miranda wakes and goes with her father to see Caliban. He enters only in response to mounting verbal abuse, which he returns with force. Prospero reminds him that he is enslaved now because, after initial harmony between them, he threatened Miranda's virginity.

Ferdinand, prince of Naples, is led on by Ariel. As he and Miranda express their sudden and mutual love, Prospero harshly overpowers him, while in asides he expresses his satisfaction with events.

Act 2 Gonzalo, with the king and others of the court party, marvels at the "miracle" of their survival and muses on the ideal commonwealth he would like to establish. Alonso mourns the loss of his son, while Antonio and Sebastian scoff at everything solemn in the others' speeches. Ariel sings Alonso and Gonzalo to sleep. Sebastian and Antonio, oblivious to Ariel's music, plot to murder Alonso and Gonzalo and usurp the throne of Naples. Ariel's music wakes Gonzalo, who, calling on "good angels," awakens the king before the plot can be implemented.

A pair of drunken clowns, Stephano and Trinculo, separated from their masters, come across the "mooncalf" Caliban and share their liquor with him. Caliban, vowing to transfer his servitude from Prospero to this foul-mouthed and grotesque pair, drunkenly leads them all offstage singing a raucous ballad of "freedom."

Act 3 Ferdinand, carrying logs at Prospero's command, and Miranda, solicitously trying to ease his burdens, speak further of their love. The forthright Miranda is the first to propose marriage. Prospero, hidden, watches with approval.

Caliban plots with Stephano and Trinculo to murder Prospero and mate Miranda with Stephano to "bring . . . forth brave brood." Ariel enters, overhears, determines to inform Prospero, and, with the tricks of a ventriloquist, turns the low rascals in confusion against each other.

Elsewhere on the island, Alonso, Antonio, and Sebastian, with others of the court party, stop to rest. To "solemn and strange music," under the direction of "Prosper on the top (invisible)," spirit-messengers bring on a banquet and invite the courtiers to feast. As, marveling, they prepare to "feed," Ariel appears "like a Harpy" to whisk the banquet away, denounce the "three men of sin," define their current experiences as fate's retribution for their injuries to Prospero, and call for their repentance and a "clear life ensuing."

Act 4   Prospero promises Miranda's hand in marriage to Ferdinand with an oblique admission he has "too austerely punish'd" him but warns the youth sternly against "break[ing] her virgin-knot" before the "full and holy rite be minister'd." Prospero orders Ariel to summon the lesser spirits to perform a wedding masque. Musicians and dancers attend Iris, the rainbow-messenger, who heralds the appearance of Juno and Ceres to confer their blessings and promises of fertility on the young lovers. The masque breaks off suddenly when Prospero remembers Caliban's plot and turns his attention to the conspirators. But first he assures Ferdinand that all is under control.

Ariel produces "glistering apparel" to be hung as temptation before the trio of base revelers. Caliban suspects trickery, but the others fight tipsily over the garments before all three are driven off by spirits in the shapes of hounds, and tormented by "dry convulsions" and "aged cramps."

Act 5   Prospero exults in his power over all that is happening. Ariel reports that the condition of the prisoners would make Prospero's "affections . . . tender"—as it would his own, "were I human." Prospero softens, and promises mercy, "the rarer action [being] / In virtue than in vengeance." He again ponders his control over the world of the spirits but promises to break his staff and drown his book when all has been accomplished. Ariel brings the courtiers into the magic circle "which Prospero ha[s] made." The magician embraces the repentant Alonso and the good Gonzalo, forgives the wrongs of Sebastian and Antonio, "unnatural" though they are, and affirms his future control over them. To a relieved and marveling Alonso, he reveals Ferdinand, with Miranda, playing chess.

Ariel returns with the ship's master and boatswain who have discovered the "split" vessel now (thanks, we learn, to Ariel's "service") fit to sail. Caliban, Stephano, and Trinculo are brought on stage. Prospero acknowledges Caliban his own and turns the others over to Alonso's control. He promises to tell the story of his life "this evening," after which all shall speed with "calm seas, auspicious gales" back home. Once the weather magic has been assured, he frees Ariel and then, alone on stage, turns to the audience to deliver the epilogue.

The Onset: Storm

For half a century now we have been led to see Shakespeare's storms in opposition to his music, the first as symbols of disorder and chaos in the human soul as well as in the macrocosm, and the second as symbolic of order and harmony, whether personal or cosmic.[4] Modern readers may have once needed to be taught this, but certain habits of symbolic thinking, no longer automatic to us, were familiar enough to Shakespeare's audiences that they would have seen much out of kilter when the action opened on a storm-tossed ship. The vessel could have signified for them either a single character, "at sea," or a social order under threat. As the scene unfolds, we see the second as more probable. Only by the end of the play do we understand that all the tangled actions on the island can be taken to represent the implicate order of Prospero's (and his creator's) mind.[5]

The first voices we hear above the storm are those of the boatswain and another sailor—busy, alarmed, but workmanlike. Then King Alonso speaks, courteously but royally condescending. The boatswain counters sharply, "I pray now, keep below." Others of the court party interrupt the mariners' labors by turns until tempers rise, all courtesy is dropped, and the passengers are forced to leave the deck. Society here is divided sharply: aboard a ship in danger, the highborn courtiers are worse than superfluous, their airs of authority meaningless. The court party is not only divided from the working mariners, it is divided itself between those who gibe and scoff at the workers, masking their fear, and those who, like Gonzalo, the king, and his son, are joined by the mariners themselves at prayers as the ship splits asunder. In retrospect we see the social and psychological divisions foreshadowing the differing responses to the educative processes the passengers will undergo when they exchange the ship for the island. The corrigible and the incorrigible among them will be subject to trials at Prospero's command, but not all will be cleansed and transformed by the baptisms they undergo.

Political Hierarchy, Usurpation, Control

A fiction set on an island "peopled" by Ariel, with his troops of fellow spirits, and by Caliban, "a salvage and deformed slave," clearly invites us to ponder an allegorical hierarchy with Prospero at the apex, above even the airy spirits he commands. Yet in the second scene, after we learn of Prospero's magical powers, we learn that he was driven all but helpless to the island when stripped of his authority as duke of Milan by his usurping brother, Antonio. Clearly this protagonist's grasp on "authority" has been shaky in the past. The whole play, as it unfolds, works out the problems associated with Prospero's authority in one sphere or another. This section deals with the overt politics in the plot; other sections will explore interconnecting issues. The figure of the good courtier occurs yet again in Gonzalo. Like Helicanus he is an old man, with a declared interest in good rule. Like Pisanio and Camillo he is unwilling to participate in his master's folly and villainy and will risk helping an intended victim. But Gonzalo goes beyond the earlier examples of his type: he questions (and ameliorates, insofar as he can) not only the act of usurpation against Prospero but later, on the island, the very principle of hierarchical rule itself. The goodness and innocence he longs for would abolish the need for laws, property boundaries, arduous labor, even weapons—all those elements in society that establish and enforce hierarchy. "All things in common Nature should produce / Without sweat or endeavour: treason, felony / Sword . . . would I not have."

Gonzalo's inconsistent picture of an ideal commonwealth may not be free of authorial irony. As the scoffers note, he "would be King" of the Edenic realm he dreams of, although all other trappings of property and authority would be unknown. Muddled or not, in his earnest confusion the good old courtier is questioning the very structures of the only kind of society he and the audience have known directly, as once he questioned the specific injustice of Alonso and Antonio and took action to save Prospero and Miranda from death at sea.

The "sin" of those conspirators, arraigned by Ariel in the guise of a harpy (3.3.53), began in sins against hierarchy in the body politic. Antonio owed fealty to his brother as rightful duke, and Alonso owed support in the alliance of states to a rightful fellow ruler. Predictably such sins led toward the murder that would surely have succeeded but for the "providential" help of Gonzalo.

Not only in Prospero's tale of the past do we see the correlation between violation of hierarchy and murder. In the dramatic present when Antonio and Sebastian plot against Alonso (2.1), the sleeping king and Gonzalo escape the conspirators' swords only through Ariel's magic music. In the parallel conspiracy against Prospero, Caliban gleefully incites his drunken companions to "brain him, / Having first seiz'd his books [the ground of his authority]; or with a log / Batter his skull, or paunch him with a stake, / Or cut his wezand."

The happy ending of the plot—which sees Prospero returning to his rightful rule in Milan, Alonso redeemed after repentance, and the youthful offspring of these benign rulers securing by marriage their fathers' renewed alliance and control over their respective states—conforms to orthodox political philosophy in the Renaissance. Only after weighing many of the interwoven issues raised by plot and poetry do we see a sanguine view of the ending as simplistic. Gonzalo's dream of Eden has opened an illogical chink into another philosophical time and place, one closer to our own, where hierarchy is seen as inviting, if not absolutely requiring, violation. The Romances question assumptions of hierarchy profoundly, as I believe other Shakespearean plays may do, but they do so ambivalently. They allow for, and superficially invite, more conventional interpretations.

Ariel: Metadrama, Magic, Alchemy

The figure of Ariel (the word *character* applied to this nonhuman spirit, agent of Prospero's magical authority over all that happens on the island, would be misleading) points us almost as directly toward the mystery of *The Tempest*'s significance as does the figure of Caliban. But not quite. It does take us quickly into the issue of Prospero's magic, far more central to this play than Cerimon's good and Imogen's stepmother's bad medicines. Considered beside Paulina's "magic," which turns out to be human stagecraft cooperating with the passage of time, Prospero's magic looks very complex.

Initially, in direct contrast to Paulina, we see Prospero as a real, not merely an apparent, magician—a learned practitioner of the ancient art of theurgy. But then as we watch him producing—through Ariel—storm, banquet, the hounding hunt, and the wedding masque, all of them illusory dramas within the drama, we see his affinity with Paulina as figure of the dramatist. We look outward from the tight circle of the fiction and the playhouse into Shakespeare's own time and ours. The magic of Prospero merges with the magic of fiction, erasing the line that divides Prospero from his maker and divides both from us as audience of their world and authors of our own. We shall return more than once to this notion of metafiction or metadrama, but now we step back into the magic circle of this island fiction to look again at Ariel.

Ariel, in more than one sense, is no angel. He shares with his predecessor, Puck, a manifest delight in the mischief he provokes, differing in that Puck's mischief is at times self-generated whereas Ariel's is always under Prospero's control. Thus even readers who have identified Caliban with the devil have hesitated to range Ariel, this agent of a human magician, above the moral level of the human. When Ariel does appear to be reading a moral lesson to Prospero (5.1.17–20), the effect is so strikingly out of character that its implications bear more on the degree of Prospero's apparently inhuman harshness than on the power of the charms he casts to move even this amoral spirit.

The one way in which Ariel does resemble a traditional angel is in his guardianship over endangered humans: he awakens Gonzalo and Alonso to save them from murder and warns Prospero when a similar plot threatens him. In neither of these good actions is Ariel under Prospero's immediate direction. In the former he stands as guardian angel under Prospero's godlike control; in the latter he stands somehow over Prospero but under some providential force that has brought him to the knowledge that will save his master. Ariel under the control of the human magician, or Ariel above him? Weighing the alternatives shakes any confidence we might initially be feeling in stable hierarchies—or in one stable prevailing philosophy—in this fictive world. It all depends on what incident we are reading and what perspective we are reading it from.

The issue here may seem isolated and trivial, but it touches on a live and ongoing debate in Shakespeare's England[6] and relates directly to one explored by Iamblichus in his treatise on ancient theurgy.[7] Is the theurgist or white magician sinning against divine power when he seeks to control persons and events by manipulating the physical elements as he does? (Ariel's name and story relate him to the higher elements of air and fire, as Caliban's story relates him to earth, and sometimes to such negative manifestations of water as the "horse-piss" through which Ariel drives the conspirators.)

Christians, in ancient and Renaissance times, were under many biblical injunctions against occult practices, all of which were suspect under church law as idolatrous and as seeking power for the magician that properly belongs only to God. Iamblichus, standing outside the early Christian tradition, argued that theurgic magic is lawful in the eyes of heaven, since the gods themselves have given the elements, and the requisite knowledge, that magicians simply employ and hand down in books like Prospero's. The argument has cogency and appeal and has been used to defend the "magic" of poetry, drama, or any form of secular learning against Puritanical opposition in many ages.[8] Shakespeare would surely stand with Iamblichus on the value and lawfulness of his own baptismal rituals, if not quite so wholeheartedly on the occult practices Prospero abandons in act 5.

Prospero's magic (like the play that is its record) seems to represent a form of alchemy—an art, science, and sometimes a form of charlatanism—that fascinated Shakespeare's society and literary contemporaries like Jonson and Donne (often satirically) even more obviously than it did Shakespeare. As there were white and black magicians, all reasonably careful to keep their activities hidden from hostile eyes, so were there scholarly, spiritually motivated alchemists and crassly corrupt charlatans preying on whatever victims they could find. Human susceptibility to power (and power claimants) being what it is, the lines were not always easy to draw between the extremes. But

Prospero, unlike Jonson's charlatan in *The Alchemist,* must be placed with the scholarly practitioners. It is these I now describe.

Within the alchemist's receptacle—island, laboratory, retort, womb, cave, magic circle (5.1.stage directions after 57), or sacred enclosure within the self—many elements contribute to, and are worked upon by, the processes that are at once natural (protochemical and psychological) and miraculous. The high is brought low into baseness, elements divide and recombine, a crucial and sacred marriage may take place between opposites. If all goes as planned, the base metal, or liquor, or soul will be transformed into gold, or life's elixir, or the "homunculus"—the little man who, more than a seed, more than a child, represents the mystery of new life exploding in the magician's consciousness. The alchemist must purify himself of all corruption if he is ever to succeed in transforming metals, potions, other human lives, or his own.[9]

Focusing back on Ariel, we find him representing one of the elemental forces that Prospero manipulates whenever he dons his magic robes. Such elementals were known to the ancient Neoplatonists as "daimons" (or "daemons") and were thought to fill a cosmos hierarchically arranged from height to depth. Within the cosmic order they could be commanded by human language and human will, for bad or good. Subject now to a white master, we remember that Ariel was once subjected by the black magic of Sycorax to imprisonment in the harder substance of a "cloven" pine (the word coupling the human witch neatly to the hoofed devil said to have fathered Caliban). Service to Prospero, however much Ariel seeks his "freedom," is clearly so much better than imprisonment in a material substance that he is ruled as much by a kind of exhilaration in his duties as by the gratitude Prospero keeps reminding him that he owes. We see a bond of affection in the relationship too, suggesting that Prospero recognizes an affinity between himself and this spirit of the higher elements that he does not feel, during most of the play, for the earthy Caliban.

One further contrast between Ariel and Caliban seems at first to be that of direct opposition. Ariel fills the island's air with the harmonious song—music and language—that so often effects the good magic; Caliban, center of disruption and chaos, sings, when he does, in drunken and profane doggerel. But the opposition is not total. When Ariel's tabor and pipe join in their scurvy song (3.2.122–30), Stephano and Trinculo are terror struck. Caliban comforts them in some of the finest poetry in the text:

> Be not afeard; the isle is full of noises,
> Sounds and sweet airs, that give delight, and hurt not.

> Sometimes a thousand twangling instruments
> Will hum about mine ears; and sometimes voices . . .
>   (3.2.133–36)

all so sweetly dreamlike to him that "when I wak'd, / I cried to dream again."

Ariel may delight in thwarting and punishing the monster on occasion, but air and earth belong somehow together in the harmony that music represents. We leave Ariel for now, to move on to the strangest, and perhaps the most powerful, element in the pattern of this play.

"This thing of darkness": Caliban

In a rich discussion of the effect of the Bermuda pamphlets and Montaigne's essay "Of Cannibals" on the play, and particularly on the figure of Caliban, Frank Kermode concludes that the "salvage and deformed slave" of the listed "Names of the Actors" represents "the natural man"—from a totally unromantic perspective.[10] Not the "noble savage" Rousseau was later to perceive in a New World Eden, this figure has links theologically to the fallen "old Adam," or as Paul calls him elsewhere, "the body of this death," who lives at the center of each of his natural descendants.

Linked as the stage has been to religious liturgy, the ignoble savage has a long history in drama.[11] Like Cloten, his closest kin in the Romances, Caliban traces his ancestry back to the Old Vice of early Renaissance folk drama and the wild man of medieval folk festivals. All of these, however grotesque and dangerous theoretically, tame the devil by making him a familiar element in dramatic entertainment. But since, familiar generically or not, Caliban is very much himself, we focus now on what he is, says, and does within the fiction.

Was he, as Prospero says, "got by the devil himself / Upon thy wicked dam"? Interpreters have conventionally taken Prospero's abusive words as explanation of the "moon-calf's" monstrosity.[12] But we have no impartial evidence on the matter. Caliban does lend support to Prospero's account of Sycorax as powerful witch, of the sort tradition accuses of consorting—often sexually—with greater or lesser devils. Estranged from Prospero when we first meet him, he angrily asserts his property right to the island his mother bequeathed him. But his subsequent words, before he falls back into a cursing that matches Prospero's, sound nostalgically sweet and anything but devilish:

> When thou cam'st first,
> Thou strok'st me, and made much of me; wouldst give me
> Water with berries in't; and teach me how
> To name the bigger light, and how the less,
> That burn by day and night; and then I lov'd thee,
> And show'd thee all the qualities of th'isle,
> The fresh springs, brine-pits, barren place and
>   fertile:
> Curs'd be I that did so!
>
>   (1.2.333–40)

This speech, his second in the play—the first being his countercurse to Prospero's abusive summons—grounds the sympathy that most audiences and readers feel for Caliban. Without it, his wild-man antics would be less entertaining; more important, the identification we feel with him, essential to any baptismal understanding of the fiction, would be impossible. Here, we sense a child of nature, open and generous toward the strangers on the island he has known as his, and presumably attractive enough before his state of "abhorred" enslavement to be "strok'd" and "made much of."

In those paradisiacal days, before the time-present of the dramatic action,[13] Caliban enjoyed from Prospero the nurture of education, as well as of foster parental affection—and as Miranda grew up, from her as well. She taught him language, which after the violent rupture in their relationship, brought him the "profit" of knowing "how to curse." That rupture, perhaps inevitable once Miranda or Caliban reached a certain minimal level of sexual maturity (he was a baby when Sycorax was banished to the island and of undefined age when Prospero arrived) resulted, Prospero says, when he attempted to "violate / The honour of my child."

Reprehensible as we find the lustful monster as he gloats at the very memory—"O ho, O ho! would't had been done!"—we should also note the implications of Prospero's words. The euphemism "honour" may be revealing more than he thinks. Had it been Miranda's physical person that alone concerned her father, the words "didst seek to violate my child" would have been clear. But the aristocratic magician, plotting to redress his own fortunes through events that will include the marriage of a virgin daughter to the son of a noble adversary, the feminine "honour" dependent on an unsullied body is all important.

Reading back to this scene, after hearing Prospero's harshly suspicious responses to Ferdinand's gestures of affection toward his betrothed (4.1.51–54), we may wonder if Caliban is a devil made, not born, shaped by a tyrannous control that has been harsher than truly required to protect the innocent daughter. [14] This notion threatens to sentimentalize the creature of an unsentimental playwright, but it arises legitimately in three contexts: in any reading that finds Caliban representing the native victims of European conquest; [15] in a comparison with the lack of horror we feel when Imogen's disguised brothers show hints of actual incestuous feeling toward the virgin who shares a family relationship with them in a pastoral setting; and in a reading that sees Caliban representing something in Prospero's own psyche, as I do in this chapter.

Meanwhile, within the fiction, Caliban knows no freedom: under Prospero's command as a menial laborer, he is subject further to the cramps and bone aches his master inflicts upon him to compel obedience. Miranda accepts her father's judgment and echoes his language:

> Abhorred slave,
> Which any print of goodness wilt not take,
> Being capable of all ill!
>   (1.2.352–54)

We sense childishly hurt feelings mixed with her acquiescence in Prospero's perspective. She says she "pitied" Caliban, taught him "each hour" to speak, and interpreted for him when his "brutish" "gabble" needed interpreting. The speech suggests a lost affection between the two. [16]

The second line does far more: it points to an understanding of Caliban's role that is basic to the richest allegorical reading. Here he sounds like *ananke,* Necessity, in Plato's account of creation in the *Timaeus,* a mysterious something like recalcitrance in matter that resists the higher shaping principle. Necessity is the dark counteragency that prevents the Demiurge, or Maker, from producing a cosmos as perfect as the Ideal Pattern he is copying. [17] Caliban as *ananke* will figure at the end of this chapter; but now, back from allegorizing to story.

It is no wonder, given his spurning by Prospero and Miranda, that Caliban transfers his allegiance to the drunken rascals who share their paltry shelter and their liquor with him in the storm Ariel has raised (2.2). Before Caliban finally (under the old coercion by torment) recognizes Prospero as the worthier master, we share quite happily in the lurching rhythms of his declaration of independence:

No more dams I'll make for fish;
    Nor fetch in firing
    At requiring;
Nor scrape trenchering, nor wash dish:
    'Ban, 'Ban, Cacaliban
Has a new master:—get a new man.
Freedom, high-day! high-day, freedom!
                (2.2.180–86)

The irony of a declaration of freedom that acknowledges a "new master" masks a profound wisdom. Those ties we choose for ourselves lead to willing service, not servitude. Freedom depends more on individual will and attitude than on outer circumstances. The theologically laden language Caliban is given in the final scene when Prospero commands his obedience invites us to think this way:

Ay, that I will; and I'll be wise hereafter,
And seek for grace. What a thrice-double ass
Was I, to take this drunkard for a god,
And worship this dull fool!
                (5.1.294–97)

He accepts the master he earlier saw as a tyrant. The language suggests more choice than capitulation: the word *ass* is there to remind us of Bottom's transformation, which, in his "eye . . . hath not heard . . . ear hath not seen" musings, moves comic dream toward mystic contemplation.[18] Behind both Bottom and Caliban stands an ancient work on magic and ritual, *The Golden Ass* of Apuleius, in which the protagonist, Lucius, is redeemed from the asshood inflicted on him by a witch when he is initiated into the mysteries of the goddess Isis.[19]

Caliban's transformation raises a chain of questions. Is he feeling simple remorse after punishment? Is he genuinely repentant—that is, sorry for what he did, not just sorry he has been caught? Can he possibly change? Can anyone?

Transformation and Christian Rituals

We have noted that Ariel and Caliban can represent, respectively, air and fire, earth and water. These original inhabitants of the magic island belong to the alchemical language woven through the text. Now, turning from the fantastic creatures of the island to the court party on whom the magician works his spells, we focus on language and incident pointing us to the central transformative rituals of European religion, the two sacraments retained by reformed Christianity, baptism and the communal banquet. When the magician (or playwright) has crucial work to do, he is likely to choose symbolic language familiar to his subjects within the fiction and to the audience beyond.

The questions raised for Caliban occur sooner or later in most human lives since, except in mythic narrative, no life runs a perfect course. If the current goal has been erroneously chosen or the aim is shaky, the result—in New Testament Greek—is *hamartia,* originally error, a missing of the target. After the errant course of linguistic development, Renaissance bibles translated *hamartia* as "sin," a far more judgmental word.

"You are three men of sin, whom Destiny . . . the never-surfeited sea / Hath caus'd to belch up" (3.3.53–56): Ariel uses biblical language to condemn Alonso, Sebastian, and Antonio, alerting them, and the audience, to their need for *metanoia,* a change of mind or direction after reflection, known in English as "repentance." The ritual that either confirms or provides the basis for *metanoia* is, in the New Testament, baptism.

The baptismal analogies in *The Tempest* begin early, in Ariel's assurances to Prospero that the ship's company has come through the storm unharmed:

> Not a hair perish'd;
> On their sustaining garments not a blemish,
> But fresher than before.
>   (1.2.217–19)

An echo of the account of the apostle Paul's shipwreck on Malta has often been noted (Acts 27:34),[20] but an even stronger chain of biblical allusions is evoked in "not a blemish." Among those figures described as unblemished are the sacrificial lambs whose blood saves the households of the Israelites at the first passover in Egypt (Exod. 12:5); the bride in the Song of Solomon (4:7; 6:9), whose virginal purity will be a willing sacrifice to her betrothed; Christ himself, as the spotless lamb of sacrifice (1 Pe. 1:19); and the church, the body and heavenly bride of Christ, sanctified and redeemed by him "with the washing of water by the word, that he might present it to himself . . . holy and without blemish" (Eph. 5:26, 27). "Not a blemish," then, of the clothes that have been through stormy seawater (their "freshness" later described by a marveling Gonzalo as "rather new-dyed than stained with salt water"

[2.1.60–62]) marks the sea change as more than an early stage in the alchemical work of transformation—as an analogue of baptism.

The distinction between magic and miracle sharpens here.[21] What is going on may well be understood by the alchemist, Prospero, as his own opus, but the audience will be alerted by the baptismal allusions to consider the work divine and to doubt the magician's claim to sole control over events. That it is the "garments," not the persons, that we see as unblemished presents no obstacle to this interpretation. Through long tradition, the garment's relation to the body has served as metaphor for the body's relation to the soul. (When the stricken Lear loosens his garments before death, the significance is unmistakable.)

The efficacy of baptism as a rite, in the ancient tradition followed by the established church in England in Shakespeare's time, does not depend on the full understanding of the one baptized. If it did, infant baptism would make no sense. Infant baptism does not guarantee salvation for the baptized: it washes off inherited taint and marks its recipients as Christ's to encourage their support in Christian community and their later awareness of available salvation. Those, once baptized, who by continuing in sin close themselves off from available grace, will be condemned. The immersion at sea can initiate in Alonso the rebaptism of the spirit that prepares him for his personal *metanoia;* can inspire in the relatively innocent Gonzalo his muddled dreams of a paradisiacal commonwealth; but it can leave the scoffers, Antonio and Sebastian, presumably more hardened in personal sin, spiritually unaffected. When Ariel's magic music separates those open to its good influence from those who simply do not hear it, it corroborates these speculations. That some of the court characters (all, presumably, as Christian Europeans, baptized) are open to the work of redemption, and some clearly not, may reflect Shakespeare's awareness of the stern Calvinistic doctrine that some are predestined to salvation and some are not. If so, the play seems to undercut that view. Caliban's final *metanoia,* with his promise that he will obey Prospero "hereafter, / And seek for grace," takes on credibility when we remember that it has been prompted by his immersion in the "filthy-mantled pool beyond [Prospero's] cell" (4.1.182) while he has been fleeing the hounds of his master's retribution. That ugly parodic baptism seems to have been enough to initiate the very necessary process of redemption for the monster we heard initially would take no "print of goodness." The *metanoia* is enough, then, to raise resistance to the stern doctrine of reprobation. If Caliban can change, who cannot?

The other of the two Protestant sacraments, the communal banquet or Eucharist, is strikingly reflected in first, the magical banquet shown the court party and whisked away to prove their ineligibility, and, second, in the wedding masque presented for Ferdinand and Miranda. In Christian liturgy the invitation to participate in the communal banquet follows a general confession of sin and an assurance of absolution. To participate in the sacramental feast when not in a humbled state of grace, of harmony with God and humanity, is regarded as all but unforgivable. In this re-presentation of the ritual, the banquet appears at first to be offered unconditionally. The unregenerate Sebastian is ready to fall to, the innocent Gonzalo has no fear, but Alonso, guilty but open to regenerative experience, senses something sacred going on and needs persuasion to approach.

By the vision of judgment, Ariel—as harpy, a classical figure of retributive justice—interrupts the conspirators. His harsh accusations of guilt both open the door to change and "guard" those accused from the wrath and perdition that await sinners and blasphemers of sacred rites by calling them to "heart-sorrow / And a clear life ensuing" (3.3.81–82). In response, the good Gonzalo marvels, not having heard the accusations; the repentant Alonso prepares to seek death with the son he believes drowned for the sin of the father; and Sebastian and Antonio, impervious to the call for repentance, prepare desperately to fight the tormenting spirits. The merciful words have done the work of judgment, have separated the relatively innocent from the guilty, and among the guilty, the apparently unregenerate from one who can and does heed the call to "heart-sorrow" and a better aim in life.

The wedding masque invites less theological commentary. The goddesses who appear before the young pair come from Olympus, not the Christian heaven that recognizes, with qualification under the reformers, only a Virgin Queen. Mary, unlike Ceres and Juno, is mother of earthly sorrows, not of joy in fertility. But the wedding masque does yield insights when interpreted against a Christian backdrop. The sense we have that these ceremonies celebrating the female and the body are faintly alien to a Christian patriarchal culture, and the fact that they are cut short when the danger represented by the earthy Caliban is remembered, start trains of thought that do not stop here.

The Virgin and the *Puer*: Miranda, Prospero, and Ferdinand

Prospero's passionate vigilance over his daughter's person leaves no room for doubting the importance of virginity as motif in *The Tempest*. Yet engaging as she is in her own girlish right, Miranda as a virginal daughter who is crucial in the process of a father's salvation pales in comparison with Marina. She is outmatched, too, by the combination of Hermione's chaste innocence and Paulina's self-assured independence, together representing the fullness of the pagan virgin as archetype. She shares nothing of the centrality of Imogen to all aspects of her play. In her ardent willingness to move beyond the virginal state into union with her princely lover, Miranda reminds us most of Perdita, another virgin daughter whose marriage unites a father with erstwhile antagonists.[22] But under her commanding father, Miranda lacks any occasion to show the command Perdita shows, far from Leontes, as mistress of the festival. Miranda's strength of will and wit as she listens to her father's long tale of their past show the potentiality of command, but father and playwright (not far apart) give her no chance to demonstrate it. With Ferdinand, we may wonder, will it be different?

Miranda's virginity, then, seems to be primarily the quality that gives her her value in a patriarchal society, not noticeably different from that of Hero in the much earlier *Much Ado About Nothing*. Miranda has little to do with the older mythic dimensions that have arisen in the images of other strong "virgins" in the Romances: the Greek virgin-goddesses defined by their independence from men; the Virgin Mary, redemptive intercessor, and mother of sorrows wherever and whenever power crucifies love. In this final Romance, the strongest emphasis has turned back on the male protagonist. That said, Prospero's daughter retains importance by the particularity of her own charms and by the ways she brings out vital characteristics in the males around her.

Miranda and Prospero are together when we first glimpse and hear them:

> If by your Art, my dearest father, you have
> Put the wild waters in this roar, allay them.
> (1.2.1–2)

The interceding virgin, quite separate from magician here in the fiction, softens the image of masculine power that has so distressed the ship's company, and with them perhaps the audience. Encountered alone, godlike power can be utterly intimidating; in conjunction with sweet compassion, its conceptual opposite, it comfortably engages our acceptance. Only gradually, as particulars accumulate in the tale he tells Miranda, do we start questioning Prospero's psychological formation in terms of the *puer-senex* pattern important in the other three Romances.

As duke of Milan, first in reputation among the heads of "the signories," the states of northern Italy, Prospero had taken all-engrossing pride in his unparalleled knowledge of the "liberal Arts," had "cast" his governing authority "upon my brother . . . Thy false uncle," remaining himself "rapt in secret studies" (1.2.70–77). This delegating of government to a regent characterized as "false" would have sounded an immediate alarm for the Jacobean audience. England would not soon forget the desperate longing for stable rule it had learned in the half-century just past. The ruler's irresponsible pursuit of his "Art" represents the rash orientation of a *puer* figure. Prospero's dereliction was worse than that of Pericles, who left the tested and true elder councillor, Helicanus, in charge as he pursued the dream of a perfect bride that parallels Prospero's alchemical search for perfection. Both *puer* driven, they seek, in the union of opposites—physical and psychic—the complement, the Anima, needed to experience the Self, to balance and complete the soul.[23]

Prospero, in Milan, should have known better. He was elder to the brother he unwisely thought fit to govern, and, as father to a three-year-old daughter, he already had known a consort, the "piece of virtue" he flippantly says assured him that Miranda was his daughter (1.2.56). Although editors explain "piece" as "model" or "masterpiece" of virtue, the hoary popular jest (so fashionable on the contemporary stage that Shakespeare even has Miranda repeat it seventy lines later) trivializes this sole mention of Prospero's inexplicably vanished wife to prompt a second look. Since the context prevents us taking the potentially derogatory word as a slur on the lady's chastity, the tone reflects badly instead on the *puer*-husband. He seems to have found, in the single-mindedness of his proud search for reputation and progeny, a virtuous spouse without ever, by the narrative present of the play, learning to name her.[24]

Whatever lack we sense in Prospero's past relationship with a "piece of virtue," we sense none in his love for Miranda. At the rough outset of his years of exile he found in his daughter "a cherubin . . . [who] did preserve me. Thou didst smile, / Infused with a fortitude from heaven." As she has matured on the island, he has found with her the ever-deepening companionship that makes him compare his "loss" of her to Ferdinand (however specious the comparison) with the "death" of Ferdinand that Alonso is grieving in the final act. If anything, we sense an incestuous surplus in his love, especially through his irascible guardianship of her virginity. Whether we take his tyrannical excesses as the function of the residual *puer* in his psyche or, as is more customary, as stemming from the tradition of the *senex* in classical drama,[25] it makes little difference to the Jungian patterns I explore in the final section of this chapter: the *puer* who is not fully integrated with the anima he so often projects on a wife, mother, or daughter, flips as he ages over to the opposite pole of the *senex,* becoming judgmental and tyrannical toward all in his control.

Turning to Ferdinand and Miranda, we know already how essential their marriage will be to the outcome of Prospero's plot—taking "plot" in all possible senses. The young lovers appear relatively seldom together, and briefly. Miranda's greater prominence in the action reflects her greater importance to Prospero, whose play this is.

As a dramatic figure, Ferdinand both possesses and seeks perfection. He serves as ideal object for the *puer* (or *puella*) side of Miranda's searching psyche: she sees him before he sees her. "What is't? a spirit?" she marvels. "I might call him a thing divine; for nothing natural / I ever saw so noble" (1.2.412, 420–22). Ferdinand's first response to the sight of Miranda matches hers[26] and fits her name, "to be admired" or marveled at: "Most sure the goddess / On whom these airs attend!" His next response brings him cannily down to earth, but still befits the *puer* in his psyche: "my prime request, / Which I do last pronounce, is, O you wonder! / If you be maid or no?" (1.2.423–30). Although the exclamation enfolded in the query softens its crassness, Ferdinand is clearly seeking an unblemished wife. Moments later he speaks his thoughts: "if a virgin, / And your affection not gone forth, I'll make you / The Queen of Naples" (1.2.450–52). At this stage, this youth would not—should circumstances require it—be capable of Posthumus's repentant grief for a wife he still believes has been "wrying just a little." Nothing indicates, of course, that the prince of Naples would ever be afflicted by the insecurity that drives the orphaned foster son of a king to murderous suspicions of his princess-bride.

Prospero, who has brought the lovers together, takes a stern and puzzling role in their first meeting. "Why speaks my father so ungently?" poor Miranda muses, probably aside. That he has been correcting Ferdinand's reference to Antonio as "duke of Milan" gives a motivation that Miranda, in context, would understand if the tone were not too immediately harsh for that. "This / Is the third man that e'er I saw; the first / That e'er I sighed for," she continues, with the prayerful wish that "my father . . . be inclin'd my way!" Innocently, with the "the first I . . . sigh'd for," she offers the interpreter a key to the father's harshness.

When Prospero imposes log-carrying labors on Ferdinand to make the "swift business" of courtship "uneasy . . . lest too light winning / Make the prize light" (1.2.453–55), Miranda's question remains with us. Normally in Renaissance romances, noble youths are sent on noble quests; Ferdinand is being asked to take over Caliban's slave labor. For Ferdinand and Miranda, the outcome is good. A *puer* humbled by menial tasks, and a virgin, eager to humble herself to share his burdens (3.1.24), are soon grounded effectively—a first step toward a less illusory sort of loving. Miranda, who certainly has more breath than Ferdinand for talking since he will not permit her to share his work, takes the lead now in offering "the jewel in her dower," her virginity, to the only "companion in the world" she can imagine wanting (2.1.54–57). With sturdy insistence she elicits his full commitment to their marriage (3.1.87) before they part.

Prospero, who has joyfully observed the growth of their "most rare affections," admits later, in brief soliloquy, "So glad of this as they I cannot be." When he explains his reservations on the basis of their surprise and his foreknowledge, we think the nobleman doth protest too much. He is about to suffer the loss of the perfect mothering daughter the *puer-senex* in his psyche has needed and, in a restrained incestuous way, treasured.

The young lovers appear in two further significant scenes, first as audience to the wedding masque, so rudely interrupted when the father-magician-dramaturge (controllers all) recalls Caliban's "foul conspiracy," whose "minute . . . Is almost come." The interruption, plausible at first, raises questions as we think about it. The threat is real, and Prospero surely has known its hour before starting the masque. Could it be that sexual undercurrents, more explicit in the dance of reapers and nymphs than in the poetry spoken by the goddesses, have reminded him of the Caliban in himself? Ferdinand certainly sees it as "strange: your father's in some passion / That works him strongly." Miranda agrees: "Never till this day / Saw I him touch'd with anger, so distemper'd." Since we know she has often seen him angry with Caliban, emphasis falls on "distemper'd." Prospero is radially off-balance.

The final appearance of the young lovers is, for one emblematic moment, a dumb show. Prospero "discovers" them to Alonso, "playing at chess." The image of affectionate contest, borne out by the brief speeches overheard by the others before Alonso and Ferdinand are reunited, neither invites nor answers the question of whether these partners, now harnessing dangerous energies by play,[27] will ever be equal. We have been permitted only the degree of interest, and knowledge, that reflects Prospero's own interest in these "pieces" he has been deploying in his own power game. But at least Ferdinand has learned Miranda's name. He knows it because the author of his circumstances, Prospero, knows it. Both delight in it precisely because it matches the "perfect and peerless" image they have seen in, while projecting it upon, the marvelous virgin (3.1.37–47).

Prospero's Transformation

Prospero's "Art" produces and governs all that unfolds in *The Tempest* until one perplexing moment in act 5. When he promises to break his staff and drown his book, Prospero proclaims and confirms a transformation in his soul effected by a magic that has plunged him "deeper than did ever plummet sound"—or this magician fathom—into the waters of his own soul. We have explored many of the stages in his inner quest; how complete his change, and in what language we may comprehend it, are questions we now confront. We focus first on the Prospero who moves within the fiction, but since the story is his, both as protagonist and as storyteller, we eventually move outward from the text to its author.

The magician's irascible nature, in evidence from the second scene and immoderate enough by the beginning of act 5 that Ariel pleads for its victims with a tenderness all but human, could be judged in many kinds of language. Aristotelians might condemn it for its excess, its deviation from the balanced mean. But Aristotle's is a philosophy that defines its norms in a very this-worldly fashion; since the magician is hardly a "normal" man, and the magic island hardly typical of this world, we move on.[28] Jesus' call to forgiveness could be brought to bear upon it: "Forgive, if ye have aught against any: that your Father also which is in heaven may forgive you your trespasses" (Mark 11:25–26); or his command and warning, "Judge not, that ye be not judged . . . with what measure ye mete, it shall be measured to you again" (Matt. 7:1–2). This is more appropriate. The "penitent humility" of Prospero's call for pardon in the epilogue marks a man who at last seems to recognize excesses for which he needs to be forgiven[29]—who has, in this sense, "repented." But how did the power-wielding magician reach that cast of mind? I propose, returning to the language Jung and the Jungians adapt from ancient drama,[30] to discuss the forces leading to Prospero's transformation in terms of the *puer-senex* polarity so evident in the male protagonists of the Romances.

I have been using the word *senex* primarily in a pejorative sense, one that fits, in the history of drama, Prospero's irascible attitude to young love. But as James Hillman has observed, the *senex* archetype is double. In its positive aspect it points to such figures as "wise old man, solitary sage, the [alchemical] *lapis* as rock of ages with all its positive . . . virtues," all of which point to positive elements we see in Prospero. Hillman points out that the good *senex* must embody many of the qualities of the *puer*—enthusiasm, compassionate femininity, the quest for spirit, the folly without which knowledge cannot be transformed into wisdom—or must assimilate such qualities to consciousness if they have been split off and submerged by the *puer*'s somersault into the *senex* role. Only the *senex-et-puer*, the full archetype, can ground the battling ego so that the Self, the fully realized soul, can emerge, and the psyche stop projecting its own unrecognized elements on surrounding persons.[31]

We have seen Prospero projecting much of himself onto both lovers and noted the primacy, in Prospero's play, of Miranda. A man captivated or transfixed by the *puer* archetype strains after an anima carrying the ideals of the spirit that first lured Prospero into the realms of secret knowledge. Many a *puer*, we have seen, roams the world in search of the perfect feminine complement, abandoning one woman after another as each proves to be limitedly human. Prospero's circumstances in *The Tempest* (as the meta-Prospero, Shakespeare, has plotted them) are different. Confined to the island, he finds in his books access to the world of the higher spirits and means of control over the lower. But the physical isolation that ensues from his self-exile to the realm of spirit limits his contact with the feminine except through Miranda. The affection he pours out on her is both incestuous, insofar as she represents to him his otherwise unknown anima, and parentally proper, since nothing indicates that he would ever act out the sexual dimension of his love if he did come to recognize it. When he inhibits Ferdinand's more appropriate ardor, he is unconsciously manifesting the safeguards that always apply to his own.

By the time present of the fiction, the very presence of the maturing Miranda has softened her father's dry ideals and stern impulses. Living, during the island years, with the virgin who bears his anima projection has gone some distance in preparing him for the culminating transformation.

Ariel too, given visible and almost palpable form by the magician's intellectual art,[32] takes on a persona of his own to relate in growing affection with Prospero. In "my delicate Ariel," "my brave spirit," and most openly in their first meeting, "Why, that's my spirit!" the terms of affection establish a bond that comes close to identity. Ariel represents, among other things, the *puer* in Prospero's psyche, submerged when the *senex* started to dominate his conscious actions. "My tricksy spirit" points to a further characteristic we have already seen in negative form in Autolycus: the restless *puer* often takes the role of the trickster—of Hermes, guide to souls in their quests for self-realization. It is Ariel, as projected trickster-*puer*, who does the actual guiding of those under Prospero's spells. When he eventually guides his master's emotions toward compassion, he merges in function not only with the compassionate virgin Miranda (as Lear's tricksy Fool merges with the compassionate Cordelia) but also with the psyche he is tutoring.

Before Ariel as a separate figure can be granted autonomy, he has had to lead that psyche, trapped in its own angry divisions as he once was trapped in the cloven pine, to the freedom available through *metanoia*. The compassion Ariel would feel were he human becomes Prospero's as soon as articulation brings it to the light of consciousness. Spirit is incorporated into soul when compassion grounds soul through awareness of its own share of darkness and sends it forth in acts of forgiveness. Once so grounded, the psyche has no further need for an externalized pure spirit as its agent.

Now back to Caliban. The eroticism of the body, along with the rashness and trickery of the negative *puer,* is often projected by a *senex*-dominated ego on what Jung calls the shadow. Hillman, after Jung, traces a human tendency to locate the shadow in monkey or ape, a beast-"man"—like the wild man, devil, or Vice of the pre-Shakespearean stage, and like Caliban.[33] He suggests that the old equation of Herakleitos, "ape is to man as man is to God" (which fits Prospero's bearing towards the monster when we first meet him), needs a further twist—"man is to God as man is to ape"—since the return to a lost likeness to God requires a "prior reunion with the fallen ape."[34] Shifting into another sort of language, we might say that the soul is saved, salved toward healing, ready to be reunited with the divine, only after the saving *metanoia,* the repentance, that accepts the Caliban within. When we know the beast in ourselves, and forgive it as we control it, we need no longer split ourselves, body against spirit, gut against head—as the vessel was splitting at the outset under the force of the tempest (1.1.61). We hold body and spirit together in the hearty wholeness of soul—greater than either, as comprehending both.[35] For that wholeness to be known, its darkness must be encountered in the struggles that no less than perfect life can escape.[36]

"This thing of darkness I / Acknowledge mine." The crowning moment in Prospero's transformation confirms the recognition of his own exorbitant harshness that Ariel earlier forced upon him. The stage Caliban of a lifetime for me, John Colicos, responded unforgettably to Prospero's words by silently unkinking his monstrously twisted body. Before our eyes the monster became human, transformed by the acceptance of one he worshipped once. Concurrently, the actor's gestural language bespoke the master's humanity.[37]

Acceptance of the shadow-Caliban baptizes the curtailed *senex*-ego into grounded selfhood. In the rash folly Caliban now confesses, as in his earlier overtures to the spotless virgin, the slavish monster has resembled a negative *puer.* (Ariel has resembled a positive. Interestingly, Ariel and Miranda never interact in the story of the play; she knows nothing of him, and he, purely spirit, needs nothing from her.) Caliban, manifesting in Prospero's play something dark in Prospero, has acted out the *puer's* incestuous desire for completion by the forbidden mother-sister-daughter and has writ large in his

vengefully murderous plotting the tendencies that Ariel checks in prompting
Prospero's realization that "the rarer action is / In virtue than in vengeance"
(5.1.27–28).

The Revels and the Epilogue

With Prospero's transformation, enacted by and with Caliban, the magician becomes a mere man: "Now my charms are all o'erthrown, / And what
strength I have's mine own, / Which is most faint." He who has been controlling a tight, relatively tidy, dramatic action on his island-stage now anticipates reentering the tempestuous human world that calls, day by day, for
responsible control, even as it continually threatens the control that it calls for.

But before we continue with the Epilogue I turn back, as promised, to the
speech that forms an epilogue of sorts to the masque Prospero has presented
to the lovers. Offering strange comfort to the "dismay'd" Ferdinand, it be-
trays the "vex'd," "troubled," "old brain" of a man caught in the upheaval he
has thought to confine to others:

> be cheerful, sir.
> Our revels now are ended. These our actors,
> As I foretold you, were all spirits, and
> Are melted into air, into thin air.
>   (4.1.147–50)

Thus far, the words make a kind of sense. Prospero is consoling Ferdinand,
"sir," for the disappearance of the actors on the grounds that they were too insubstantial to be seriously missed. (Miranda seems to be forgotten, but perhaps she is too used to her father's pranks to be disturbed.) But then Prospero
negates the consolation:

> . . . like the baseless fabric of this vision,
> The cloud-capp'd towers, the gorgeous palaces,
> The solemn temples, the great globe itself,
> Yea, all which it inherit, shall dissolve,
> And, like this insubstantial pageant faded,
> Leave not a rack behind.
>   (4.1.151–56)

If Ferdinand has been "dismay'd" to lose the vision promising an earthly paradise for himself and his bride, he now is asked to contemplate an apocalypse ending the world he so substantially enjoys in the rapture of new love.

The process of dissolution continues, in "we" denying the corporeality of speaker and listener—and by extension outward, of actors on Shakespeare's stage, and of those who watch them play at living:

> We are such stuff
> As dreams are made on; and our little life
> Is rounded with a sleep.
> (4.1.156–58)

The age-old philosophic commonplaces, that life is to death as day is to sleep, and that this world is less real than some otherwhere, dissolve in some confusion as "dreams" on one plane of the metaphor meet "sleep" on the other. Prospero is astute enough to break off now with excuses for his troubled old brain. His auditors, Ferdinand and Miranda speaking as one, wish him "peace," leaving him to walk "a turn or two . . . To still" his "beating mind." The little epilogue to the masque is a microcosm of the Epilogue Prospero speaks as he steps out of the fiction at the end of act 5.

Before returning to that, we note that the fiction breaks off with a promise of more story. Prospero will "deliver all" of his story to Alonso—as Leontes commanded his companions, and as Pericles requested Cerimon, to do. Each of these plays promises to loop back, to replay what the audience has already seen and heard.[38] *Cymbeline* is the exception. All its stories are retold, all ends neatly tied, in the hilariously busy final act that comes to final rest in the proclamation of the peace that points to the birth at distant Bethlehem. The beginning of the Christian story supersedes, and wraps up, *Cymbeline*'s other stories, effecting there, at least, the harmony missing in most human affairs.

The Epilogue the Prospero-actor addresses to the audience for the Prospero-playwright looks forward, not back, and its shifting tones contrast sharply with the final words he speaks before stepping out of his controlling, and self-controlled, character: to the court party "I'll . . . promise you calm seas, auspicious gales"; to "My Ariel, chick . . . Be free, and fare thou well!"; to the audience, in transition, "Please you, draw near."

The first lines of the actual Epilogue are ambivalent: "Now my charms are all o'erthrown, / And what strength I have's mine own" could be delivered confidently, but the voice must falter on "Which is most faint." The speech proceeds with an admission and a plea that moves outward from Prospero's

fiction to the predicament of an actor seeking the applause that will release
him from his role on the now "bare" island-stage:

> I must be here confin'd by you,
> Or sent to Naples. Let me not,
> Since I have my dukedom got,
> And pardon'd the deceiver, dwell
> In this bare island by your spell;
> But release me from my bands
> With the help of your good hands

The transition from character to actor is, however, unsteady. It is the actor
who would be "confin'd" (like Ariel) without "good hands"; but it is the
character he has played who has regained a dukedom by the magic that is
now, in "spell," given over to the audience, and the character who, in the
simply humanity to which his own actor-spirit Ariel has recalled him, has
conferred the pardon. As our minds play over the implications, it is, curi-
ously, Prospero, the character, with whom we finally identify in the human
need for liberation from our "bands." Yet what is that bondage, ultimately,
we are left wondering.

The next lines bespeak the actor:

> Gentle breath of yours my sails
> Must fill, or else my project fails,
> Which was to please.

But not just the actor. Each of us, caught in our human "faintness" in the web
of relationships, and strand by strand relying on our power to please others to
gain release, must enact a similar role. "Breath" and "sails" take us further
into mystery. In both Hebrew and Greek the words for breath, wind, and
spirit are identical: such is the power of metaphor to compress the notions of
breath of life, breath of the cosmos, and breath of God. *Anagoge,* the
Neoplatonists' term for the mystical elevation of the spirit sought by participants in Plotinian dialectic and Iamblichan ritual, is a metaphoric word that
originally meant the hoisting of sails to catch the wind before setting to sea.
The words bring into play all levels of the soul, the physical in the implied sea
voyage, the social in the acknowledgment of interdependence, the spiritual in
"breath," and the expectancy of waiting sails.

Next we are turned back into the magician's story: "Now I want / Spirits
to enforce, Art to enchant; / And my ending is despair." The magician with-

out his art is mere man, an Everyman; we all, potentially, need the rescue from despair now indicated, a relief "by prayer, / Which pierces so, that it assaults / Mercy itself, and frees all faults."

If the audience (and each reader as its extension) has not already been fully engaged in the participatory mimesis of which I spoke in the introductory chapter, the final two lines command it. They link theatrical performance to secular life and reciprocal human goodwill to hope for the ultimate pardon: "As you from crimes would pardon'd be, / Let your indulgence set me free."

By this time in our experience of *The Tempest* (and the other Romances) most boundaries—between the magician's and the playwright's art, theatrical fiction and life, life and life beyond—have been so eroded that we share Prospero's uncertainties and hopes in almost equal measure. Like him, when the play is over, we face continuing stories in which the endless interplay between light and dark, spirit and body, masculine and feminine, theatrical posing and authentic action, will go on. Our lives move through tempests that yield to baptismal flashes of self-knowing and eventually calmer seas, but any human promise of "calm seas, auspicious gales" must be held in doubt.

Whether we hear the confession of incipient despair as Prospero's, the actor's, Shakespeare's, or our own, will depend on the degree of participatory mimesis we are experiencing. The art of the playwright demands the vital interpretation of actor and audience or reader. Whether the traditional happy ending, or the qualified hope offered in the Epilogue can long satisfy depends too on our participatory goodwill (the suspension of disbelief, the breath of ours that fills the dramatic sails). That, in turn, depends on the current tone of our ongoing lives.

Prospero's (the actor's? the playwright's?) quavering call for release fits the nature of the genre he has inhabited. The inescapable quest defines romance. Its ground, its necessary condition, is the dangerous freedom that calls, toward the end, for the release Caliban finds in his *metanoia,* his reconciliation with the fallible god he now knows as better than a recently known alternative.[39]

Chapter Six
"Tell thy story": An Afterword

As his sonnets repeatedly remind us, no concluding word on Shakespeare's Romances can be written "so long as men can breathe" and read, and a poet's "black lines" continue to offer a counterthrust to "Age's cruel knife."[1] But we can consider the progress of these plays through history and their continuing importance in our own theaters and lives.

Snatches of Their Histories

The disdain of Shakespeare's rival, the "realistic" playwright Ben Jonson, for "mouldy tales" peopled by monsters and structured on improbable plot devices did not, certainly, reflect the taste of contemporary audiences. So far as we can tell, each of the Romances enjoyed enough success in contemporary theaters to justify fully the commercial Shakespeare's enterprise in writing them. From the time of the closing of the theaters under the Commonwealth to Romantic and Victorian times, tastes antithetical to the Romances prevailed. Only *The Tempest* can boast continued popularity with audience and critics through every century subsequent to first performance.[2]

Pericles was popular with early-seventeenth-century audiences but was never performed from the time of the Restoration until 1738 when a rewritten version, Lillo's *Marina,* was staged at Covent Garden. A version staged at Sadler's Wells in 1854 expurgated most of the brothel scenes and omitted Gower. Thus tailored to Victorian tastes it enjoyed a run of some weeks. But for most of the eighteenth and nineteenth centuries, the play was excluded from the Shakespeare canon as a poor thing in which he probably had little part. This century has been different, at least since 1920. Productions have been mounted in most of the major Shakespeare centers in the world: the Stratfords of England, Ontario, and Connecticut; the Old Vic and National Theatre stages in London; Paris; Ashland, Oregon—to name only a few. In 1986, *Pericles* figured in the revival of the three lesser-known Romances at Stratford, Ontario, in a striking production featuring a female black singer as Gower. The conventionality of gospel rock, which echoed through her music, worked splendidly for Gower's conventional choruses. The Pericles of that production, played by Geraint Wyn Davies, provides the image of the *puer aeternus* that constitutes the frontispiece to this book. Even more recently, Peter Hall included *Pericles* in his revival of the Romances at the National Theatre in England. *Pericles,* stark, romantic, and realistically lewd, seems to have found its century with us.

Cymbeline, similarly, was popular with Jacobean audiences, who would be pleased by its topical references and its nationalism. Also like *Pericles,* it was misunderstood and disliked through the classical period in England but regained its popularity with the Romantics. Its reputation has fluctuated since then, but only since World War II has it been produced frequently. More than the others, this very long play is vulnerable to a director's decisions on cutting, as it is also on the staging and acting of the scene wherein Imogen awakes to the nightmare of Cloten's headless body, arguably as grotesque as anything else in Shakespeare. Shakespeare's lines, even truncated, are dramatically secure enough to survive most decisions taken in modern productions, but rarely can a single staging satisfy a lover of the complex text by capturing both its romance and its irony. A good production must reveal the pathos of Imogen's initiation without provoking too many nervous giggles; it should, however, please by provoking a happy, disbelieving, hilarity by playing the final scene at breakneck speed.

The Winter's Tale, like its fellows, was popular to 1640. It then sank out of sight until a performance in 1740. Much altered versions were staged in the second half of the eighteenth century: the pastoral scenes featuring Autolycus's roguery were surefire in an age of classicism and satire. Nineteenth-century audiences loved the play, especially for Hermione—a model Victorian wife. During our century it has continued to prove popular.

The Tempest has enjoyed uninterrupted popularity since its first staging. Its strict observance of the classical unities protected it from censure during the eighteenth century; the nineteenth century loved it for the allegory and the autobiography perceived in it. Our century has admired it for, in addition to its supreme playability, the complexity of its intellectual patterning. And perhaps instinctively, current audiences and readers respond to the Caliban who figures forth so much in human experience that a period moving away from conventional theology needs to locate somewhere. We now love the monster more readily than we fear him. Like the monsters of our children's pop culture, Caliban's popularity is secure.

All four Romances have found deserved prominence in our late-twentieth-century theaters. They are similarly popular in academic curricula and among those who continue to read Shakespeare for pure enjoyment. The stories they tell, the transformations they play out on stage and page, will continue to work their way into any imagination open to them. These stories can transform our own if we let them.

Glimpses of Our Own

Our inner lives may manifest the truest stories of all, but until we face and accept them as our own they may seem, like the myths and folktales that mirror them, the worst of delusions. So, too, may the dreamlike events we actually encounter in waking life—those that break through mysteriously to the deepest self.

"This is the rarest dream that e'er dull'd sleep / Did mock sad fools withal" murmurs a bewildered Pericles as Marina summons him out of his own dream of despair. But when he knows his daughter as his own, he wakes to the refreshing winds of change. "My life stands in the level of your dreams," Hermione protests to Leontes; but he, denying the reality of her goodness, takes his nightmares as her "actions." When those nightmares are undone by the "spell" of Paulina, he cries, "If this be magic, let it be an art / Lawful as eating." Dreaming, the satisfaction of appetites, an art that spells in the magic of language: all intertwine in Leontes' plea. And from his new happiness he turns, with his court, to the retelling of happy tales.

We, participating in the fantastic mimeses of living that these Romances unfold for us, share in Leontes' plea. We want to feed our insufficient selves by the power of verbal and ritual art, and we want to find the art "lawful"—in keeping with the natural law of the world we inhabit. We would like these stories of the Romances to fit the stories we construct about the events we enjoy and endure.

Unlike Prospero, who as magician stands so close to Shakespeare in our imaginations, we rarely have full control over our experiences; we cannot always intervene like gods from the upper machinery to manifest our most fertile and harmonious dreams. But we can dream on: "we are such stuff as dreams are made on," and with or without a magician's charms we can hope for release from the nightmares of the day. Such hope the Romances have set before us in all beauty, and in some terror. They entice us to incorporate their substance into the patterns of our own innerness—patterns conforming to the cycles of ancient fertility myths and to the redemptive myths of the Bible. But like the slippery language by which they reach us, they keep dissolving from our grasp.

I claim no more finality for the past four chapters, my stories of four plays, than that they reflect, as well as I could make them reflect, the truths I experienced in the texts in the evanescent now of writing. After the next production I see of any one of them, the next time I teach any one of them, the next tempest or wintry tale I live through, the truths I see may manifest new shapes.

What about you? Life has a way of imitating the stories with which we identify. What stories will you find, or choose, to give shape to your dreams and to the actualities you experience? Do you see yourself in Othello or Leontes? in Lear or Prospero? in Hermia, Miranda, or Desdemona? in Hermione, Paulina, or Perdita? in Ariel, Caliban, or both? Shakespeare holds out stories in the many shapes of history, comedy, tragedy, and Polonius's mixtures—but in these tragicomedies he gives his all but final words. These Romances, these dreams, offer models of transformation and comfort, and in their open endings the discomfiture of radical freedom.

Notes and References

Chapter One

1. For convenience throughout this book, Shakespeare's romances, when referred to without the author's name preceding the word, are indicated by a capital on "Romances." Lowercase "romance(s)" refers to the genre at large or to other romances.

2. Studies linking Jacobean history to the Romances include Frances Yates, *Shakespeare's Last Plays* (London: Routledge and Kegan Paul, 1975), Jonathan Goldberg's *James I and the Politics of Literature* (Baltimore: Johns Hopkins University Press, 1983), and David Bergeron, *Shakespeare's Romances and the Royal Family* (Lawrence: University Press of Kansas, 1985).

3. For the representative incidents summarized here see, in Heliodorus, *An Aethiopian Romance,* trans. Thomas Underdowne (rev. F. A. Wright, London: George Routledge & Sons, n.d.), 190, 230, 245.

4. *Cosmos and History* (New York: Harper, 1958) is representative of Mircea Eliade's work in this vein. G. Wilson Knight, *The Shakespearian Tempest* (London: Methuen, 1953), demonstrates the pervasiveness of such patterns throughout the plays.

5. Eliot's words may not have been in the designer's mind, but they must have occurred to more than one in the audiences for that production.

6. Johnson's remark is quoted by J. M. Nosworthy in his introduction to the *Cymbeline,* Arden Shakespeare (London: Methuen, 1963), xli. Subsequent citations are provided parenthetically in the text.

7. See 1 Sam. 28 for the story.

8. The Iamblichus text was widely available in Ficino's Latin translation in the Renaissance, usually published in a volume including the hermetic tracts and works by Proclus and Psellus. One such edition is *Iamblichus De mysteriis Aegyptorum, Chaldorum, Assyriorum. Proclus in Platonicum Alcibiadem de anima, atque daemone. Idem De sacrificio, & magia. Porphyrium De diuinis atq. daemonibe. Psellus De daemonibus. Mercurii Trismegisti Pimander. Eiusdem. Asclepius* (Lvggdvni: apud Ioan Tornaesivm 1570).

For the magic working of Ficino, see D. P. Walker, *Spiritual and Demonic Magic from Ficino to Campanella* (Notre Dame: University of Notre Dame Press, 1975), and of Dee, see Peter French, *John Dee, the World of an Elizabethan Magus* (London: Routledge and Kegan Paul, 1972). For the rivalries between Christian and Neoplatonic devotees see R. T. Wallis, *Neoplatonism* (London: Duckworth, 1972), 128–29.

9. Among those who have recently studied the importance of Renaissance

magic to the plays of Shakespeare and his contemporaries are: Charles Nicholl, *The Chemical Theatre* (London: Routledge & Kegan Paul, 1980); Barbara Traister, *Heavenly Necromancers: The Magician in English Renaissance Drama* (Columbia: University of Missouri Press, 1984): and David Woodman, *White Magic and English Renaissance Drama* (Cranbury, N. J.: Associated University Presses, 1971).

10. Nicholl, *Chemical Theatre,* xx.

11. *The Winter's Tale,* ed. J. H. P. Pafford, Arden Shakespeare (London: Methuen, 1955), 4.4.88. Subsequent references to this edition are cited parenthetically in the text.

12. What follows here is abridged from the introductory chapter of my recent book, *Plato Baptized: Towards the Interpretations of Spenser's Mimetic Fictions* (Toronto: University of Toronto Press, 1988). Perkins is quoted from *The Work of William Perkins,* ed. Ian Breward (Appleford: Sutton-Courtenay Press, 1970), 377–78. The term "personal knowing" is adapted from Michael Polanyi's *Personal Knowledge: Towards a Post-Critical Philosophy* (Chicago: University of Chicago Press, 1968).

13. Perkins, 162–63 and 377–78.

14. *King Lear,* ed. Kenneth Muir, Arden Shakespeare (London: Methuen, 1952), 1.1. 158–59.

15. The centrality of this concept to the Romances in the context of seastorms and sea change is demonstrated in later chapters.

16. A much fuller account of the Renaissance thinking that derived from the Greeks and the Bible can be found in the first five chapters of my *Plato Baptized.*

17. The "recovery" may be of a fiction; that is, the memory may have more to do with the child's memory-record of fears and imaginings than with any actual event.

18. Etymologically the following words are connected: whole, hale, heal, health; salve, salvation, save.

19. "An Anatomy of the World: The First Anniversary," 11. 464–66. One available edition is *John Donne: The Complete English Poems,* ed. A. J. Smith (Harmondsworth: Penguin, 1971).

20. The phrase is Shelley's ("Ode to the West Wind"); Wordsworth's conviction that memory is that which binds the child and the man together in the human soul shapes *The Prelude.*

21. See Carl Jung, *Modern Man in Search of a Soul* (New York: Harcourt, Brace & World, 1933), 16–19, 115–24.

22. For clarification of these and other terms, Aniela Jaffe provides a useful glossary in *Memories, Dreams, Reflections: C. G. Jung* (London: Collins and Routledge and Kegan Paul, 1964), 349–57.

23. *C. G. Jung Speaking,* ed. William McGuire and R. F. C. Hull (London: Pan, Picador, 1980), 49.

24. Jung, *Modern Man in Search of a Soul,* 172.

25. Eric Neumann, *Art and the Creative Unconscious* (New York: Harper & Row, 1966), 119–25.

26. A fuller elaboration of this term may be found in my *Plato Baptized,* 17–18. Although he does not use my terminology, A. D. Nuttall's thinking in *A New Mimesis, Shakespeare and the Representation of Reality* (London: Methuen, 1983) (which I did not read until after my own theories were formulated) is compatible with them. His arguments, of course, are grounded in much the same literature as my own.

27. Hans-Georg Gadamer in *Truth and Method* (New York: Crossroads, 1985), 97–108, 124–27, traces ways in which representation came to mean re-presentation.

Chapter Two

1. I am indebted to several careful and extensive discussions of these issues, and especially so to F. D. Hoeniger's introduction to his Arden edition of *Pericles* (London: Methuen, 1963) and to J. C. Maxwell's introduction to the Cambridge edition (Cambridge: At the Press, 1956).

2. As my student a few years ago let it happen to him. See chapter 1.

3. I follow a distinction between *story,* a mere relating of incident, and *plot,* a retelling of story in which deeper structures and connections reveal meaning. In this sense, the rest of this chapter deals with *plot*—after the story has been reviewed.

4. Ben Jonson's peevish dismissal of *Pericles* as a "mouldy play" is quoted in Hoeniger's introduction, 1xix.

5. See "The Uncanny," in Sigmund Freud, *Complete Psychological Works* (London: Hogarth Press, 1955), 17: 217–52. "Uncanny" translates the word *unheimlich,* which converges on the positive form, *heimlich* (familiar and agreeable), when familiar matters that "ought to have remained secret and hidden . . . come to light" (225).

6. Ibid., 244–46.

7. This is not the place to review the literary issues raised by the book of Job. I do scrutinize them in my *Plato Baptized,* 63–69.

8. Hoeniger, in his introduction to the Arden *Pericles,* looks at this connection. Anne Righter in *Shakespeare and the Idea of the Play* (London: Chatto and Windus, 1964) and A. P. Rossiter in *English Drama from Early Times to the Elizabethans* (London: Hutchinson University Press, 1950) give valuable background information.

9. At the Stratford (Ontario) Festival, 1987.

10. See chapter 1 on alchemy.

11. E. M. W. Tillyard in *The Elizabethan World Picture* (London: Chatto and Windus, 1964) and C. S. Lewis in *The Discarded Image* (Cambridge: Cambridge University Press, 1964) give standard descriptions of the world of interconnecting analogies visualized in traditional Renaissance thinking.

12. *King Richard II,* ed. Peter Ure, the Arden Shakespeare (London: Methuen, 1956) 3.2.156. Subsequent references to this edition are cited parenthetically in the text.

13. My adjustment to the text reflects most editors' sense that here the reporter was particularly lax, but however the line was scrambled, the moral intention is clear.

14. *Plato: The Collected Dialogues, including the Letters* (Princeton: Princeton University Press, 1961, 1973), ed. Edith Hamilton and Huntington Cairns 1574–98.

15. Full title: *The First Blast of the Trumpet against the Monstrous Regiment of Women* (One modern edition:New York: DaCapo Press, 1972).

16. For an opposing reading, see Bergeron, *Shakespeare's Romances,* 122–24.

17. To forge bonds of friendship and obligation in aristocratic and higher professional circles, children of one family might be sent at a tender age to live and be educated in another family. See Lawrence Stone, *The Family, Sex and Marriage in England, 1500–1800* (London: Weindenfield and Nicolson, 1977), for further information on fostering.

18. Marianna L. Novy in *Love's Argument: Gender Relations in Shakespeare* (Chapel Hill: University of North Carolina Press, 1984) and Stevie Davies in *The Idea of Woman in Renaissance Literature: The Feminine Reclaimed* (Brighton: Harvester, 1986) are among the many in the last decade who have worked with such gender differentiation in Shakespeare.

19. *Macbeth,* ed. Kenneth Muir, the Arden Shakespeare (London: Methuen, 1957), 4.3.204–21.

20. Nicholl, *Chemical Theatre,* 75, calls this speech "a Paracelsian manifesto."

21. Hoeniger, Introduction, 3, notes that the "ceremony" associated with Cerimon in both his scenes "is . . . reflected in Prospero's emphasis in holy 'ceremony' when addressing Ferdinand in the fourth act of *The Tempest.*"

22. I am indebted in the preceding paragraphs to the early pages of Marie Louise von Franz's *Puer Aeternus* (Santa Monica: Sigo Press, 1981).

23. Julia Kristeva in *Tales of Love* (New York: Columbia University Press, 1987), 222, notes that in a good marriage, "if the couple truly becomes one, . . . each of the protagonists . . . has married his or her mother." The point is that the completion of the self in the other in marriage satisfies the incestuous hunger left when the primal unity between mother and child is broken.

Von Franz is quoted from *Puer Aeternus,* 24.

24. For "switching," see von Franz in *Puer Aeternus,* 2.24. For the *senex's* relationships to the *puer* and to Saturn, see James Hillman, "Senex and Puer," in his *Puer Papers* (Irving, Texas: Spring Publications, 1979).

25. See Marina Warner, *Alone of All Her Sex* (New York: Alfred A. Knopf, 1976), and M. Esther Harding, *Woman's Mysteries* (New York: Harper & Row, 1971).

26. Helena's healing of the king in *All's Well That Ends Well* demonstrates Shakespeare's familiarity with this archetypal motif.

27. The "virginal" autonomy and power arising from a woman's integration with her body is the subject of Marion Woodman's *The Pregnant Virgin* (Toronto: Inner City Books, 1985).

28. The fresh garments look ahead to the baptismal freshness of the sea-washed garments of the ship's company in *The Tempest,* Frank Kermode, ed., Arden Shakespeare (London: Methuen, 1954), 2.1.59–62. Subsequent references to this edition are cited parenthetically in the text.

Chapter Three

1. Tennyson, dramatically arranging the scene of his own death, commanded that his Shakespeare be opened at that page so that his dying hand could rest upon it. The beauty he found in it was surely a comfort to the Victorian Lady Tennyson. It would prove less so to most wives this hundred years later. See Hallam, Lord Tennyson, *Alfred, Lord Tennyson, a Memoir,* (London: Macmillan, 1897), 776.

2. See J. M. Nosworthy's Introduction to *Cymbeline,* the Arden Shakespeare, (London: Methuen, 1955) xii–xxix, for fuller discussion of the issues I touch on in this section. All quotations from *Cymbeline* are from this edition. The comment below on romance sources is from xxvi.

3. See Goldberg, *James I and the Politics of Literature* (Baltimore: Johns Hopkins University Press, 1983), and Bergeron, *Shakespeare's Romances and the Royal Family* (Lawrence: University Press of Kansas, 1985).

4. Some productions cut the very long final scene to eliminate the impression of the playwright's complicated contrivance, but to do that is to miss the point entirely. The playwright stands to this play in the same relation as the author of the world to his creation. The very joy in living of the characters depends on the sense of the miraculous that their experiences have given them here. One of the best productions I have seen played it almost as a conscious parody of romance, at breakneck speed. The laughter that the tumbling of the revelations generated was laughter of relief, of joy, as well as a sophisticated laughter at the craftsmanship of author, director, and players.

5. This is not to suggest that Braggadocchios and more uncanny monsters like Orgoglio (both, of course, in Spenser's *Faerie Queene*) do not belong in the romance genre but that they, like Cloten, enter the pastoral fictions to define their effects by contrast.

6. See chapter 2.

7. Rossiter, *English Drama,* Righter, *Shakespeare,* provide information and insights to this sort of drama.

8. See chapter 2, note 17.

9. That tension existed that far back between Britain and its conqueror, Rome, need not cancel the queen's guilt in forcing the denial of tribute. The uneasy

political situation was not, at least nominally, that of complete subjection but rather that of a covenant between a weaker and a more powerful nation.

10. See chapter 2.

11. I elaborate on this metaphor in Spenser in *Plato Baptized,* chap. 8.

12. The tales of Arthur, Lancelot, and Guinevere demonstrate that a king will be judged by the reputations of his courtiers, as the husband is by his wife's. The sin against the royal marriage bed by Lancelot, the king's foremost knight, is as destructive to Camelot as that of the queen herself.

13. In Plato's *Timaeus* (69e), the Maker sets the neck as "isthmus and boundary" between the pure and all-important head and the body that threatens to pollute it. The hierarchical symbolism there revealed and established has been a threat to woman as earthy body in traditional thinking ever since.

14. The attitude goes back at least as far as that ancient love poem, the Song of Solomon: "Thou are all fair, my love," sings the bridegroom, "there is no spot in thee" (4:7). The symbolism underlies the symbolism of the red spots on the white handkerchief that Othello takes as evidence of Desdemona's sexual taint. Neoplatonism does not help the cause of less than perfect women: it holds that true bodily beauty reflects true spiritual beauty. Although Neoplatonists recognize that false beauty may deceive the beholder, in practice physical imperfection in a woman may not be given the benefit of the doubt.

15. Lisa Jardine, in *Still Harping on Daughters* (Brighton: Harvester Press, 1983), devotes her first chapter to "female roles and Elizabethan eroticism."

16. We hear, if attentive, an echo of the New Testament tale of the boy Jesus' learning which so astonished the elders at the temple on his twelfth birthday (Luke 2:46–52).

17. See footnote in the Arden edition, 141, for an example.

18. I am not trying to make a full "Christ figure" out of Imogen here, and certainly not out of the body she embraces, which is Cloten's, after all. But the shapes of Christian myth, as they emerge from biblical intertexts, do enrich as analogues our understanding of the Romances.

19. See Neumann, *The Great Mother,* 31.

20. In an introductory commentary to act 5, Arden edition, 152.

21. *Othello,* ed. M. R. Ridley, the Arden Shakespeare (London: Methuen, 1965), 3.366. The "pearl" image derives from Othello's own words (5.2.348).

22. This movement of the text conforms to the biblical wisdom that "whosoever will save his life shall lose it: and whosoever will lose his life for my sake shall find it." If we interpret "for my sake," justifiably, as "for the sake of love," we see the intertextual connections.

23. We remember here that the eagle was associated with Posthumus when Imogen contrasted him to Cloten as "puttock."

24. James Hillman is chief among those post-Jungians who propose "that we aim less at gathering the sparks [of psychic consciousness] into a unity and more at integrating each spark [into consciousness] 'according to its own principle.'" I quote

here from Andrew Samuels, *Jung and the Post-Jungians* (London: Routledge & Kegan Paul, 1985), 107. The internal quotation is from Hillman.

25. See footnote in Arden edition, 167.

26. Christopher Fry's words, first published in *Vogue*, January 1951, are reprinted in *Comedy: Meaning and Form*, ed. Robert W. Corrigan (San Francisco: Chandler, 1965), 15–17.

27. As my student found when the magic of *Pericles* carried over, for him, to the next day and the next lecture hour. See chapter 1.

Chapter Four

1. Robert W. Uphaus draws distinctions similar to these in *Beyond Tragedy: Structure and Experience in Shakespeare's Romances* (Lexington: University Press of Kentucky, 1981). J. H. P. Pafford, editor of the Arden edition of *The Winter's Tale* (London: Methuen, 1963), finds a high degree of realism in Leontes' mad jealousy and other points of characterization—more than I do. (All quotations from the play are from this edition.) Howard Felperin in "Tongue-tied our queen?': The Deconstruction of Presence in *The Winter's Tale*," in *Shakespeare and the Question of Theory*, ed. Patricia Parker and Geoffrey Hartman, (New York: Methuen, 1985), 3–18, discusses the contribution of intricate language to the lifelike slipperiness we encounter in the play.

2. The probable contribution of Greene's "cony-catching" pamphlets to the character of Autolycus is discussed by Pafford in his Introduction, xxxiv–v.

3. Pafford, in section 4 of his Introduction (lxiii—lxvii), discusses the interrelationships at length as they have been defined by critics over the years.

4. Pafford's introduction deals with the "structural mare's nests . . . [as] nonexistent problems" throughout, but especially li–lv.

5. In the absence of firm proof for any speculation on text and date, the summaries of textual issues given in the Arden introductions for each of these plays give acceptable guidance—although bibliographical debates continue in the literature.

6. Romano was an actual Renaissance sculptor. This notorious "anachronism," of course, is one of many devices in this play blurring the boundaries between art and life.

7. Felperin, "Tongue-Tied Our Queen?" finds, as I do, that Hermione is probably innocent but that Leontes' suspicions have more than a little foundation in the ambiguities of the text.

8. *Measure for Measure*, ed. W. Lever, the Arden Shakespeare (London: Methuen, 1965), 1.4.29.

9. Camillo's word recalls the Platonic distinction between *truth*, which accords with the eternal patterns, and *opinion*, which is precariously based on the evidences of fallible human sense.

10. We note a contrast here to *Cymbeline* wherein slander attacks the royal Imogen from outside the family.

11. Jardine, *Still Harping on Daughters*, notes the equation of a talkative

woman with witchery, shrewishness, and other evils in the Renaissance. See especially chaps. 2 and 4.

12. The broader theoretical premises for this book have been sketched in my introductory chapter, but here it is important to review them.

13. See Righter, *Shakespeare and the Idea of the Play*, passim.

14. Although I have begun by using the Jungian and post-Jungian terminology of the *puer*, since so much that Marie von Franz and Hillman have observed is applicable, the insights of Freud are basic to the same psychological mechanisms, and those of the post-Freudian Lacan about a "fall" into ambiguous language are particularly applicable to the occasions of Leontes' judgments. For elaboration, see, in addition to works cited in chapter 2, Stephen Frosh, *The Politics of Pychoanalysis: An Introduction to Freudian and Post-Freudian Theory* (New Haven: Yale University Press, 1987), chaps. 6, 7.

15. The ensuing discussion is prompted by Hillman's *Puer Papers*. For the late-ancient and medieval currency of the *puer-senex* topos—and thus its availability to Shakespeare—see E. R. Curtius, *European Literature and the Latin Middle Ages*, trans. Willard R. Trask (Princeton: Princeton University Press, 1973), 98–101.

16. This paragraph and the next quote and paraphrase James Hillman's "Senex and Puer" in *Puer Papers*, 24, 25.

17. The phrase is from ibid., 19. The whole paragraph is indebted to "Senex and Puer."

18. Milton's phrase (Sonnet 23), expresses the age-old patriarchal taboos upon the blood mysteries of womanhood. Such taboos gave rise to the Levitical law prescribing purification after childbirth and persisted in Milton's day in the Anglican ritual of "churching" a new mother. The other quotation is adapted from Polixenes' opening speech (1.2.1).

19. Many of the insights here run parallel to those of Coppélia Kahn in "The Providential Tempest and the Shakespearean Family" in *Representing Shakespeare*, ed. Murray M. Schwartz and Coppélia Kahn (Baltimore: Johns Hopkins University Press, 1980). Kahn's chosen terminology is more Freudian than mine: my choice of the "puer" archetype, codified by Jungians, was suggested, of course, by Shakespeare's own phrase, "boy eternal."

20. Again Lisa Jardine in *Still Harping on Daughters*, 181–94, is instructive. She traces the "nobility in adversity" Renaissance writers habitually located in figures like Griselda and Lucrece.

21. The *Oxford English Dictionary* derives "hermeneut" or interpreter from the name of Hermes, whom the Romans called Mercury. Other attributes of this young god, messenger of the greater gods—trickiness, speed in constant journeying, inconsistency—signal his importance in any exploration of *puer* psychology like this play.

22. See "Notes on Opportunism" in Hillman, *Puer Papers,* esp. 159, 161, 163.

23. The male nipple, "mamma," takes a different vowel in the second syllable.

24. See Pafford's Introduction, lxxxii.

25. I am thinking here, of course, of the dark and bloody atmosphere of Macbeth's Scotland. Kahn, "The Providential Tempest and the Shakespearean Family," sees the death of Mamillius in much the same way as I do.

26. According to Robert Graves' commentary on the Homeric character in *The Greek Myths* (Harmondsworth: Penguin, 1955), 5.2, 64–70, 274, 348.

27. In addition to Graves, I have consulted a Greek lexicon and the *Oxford English Dictionary* for this paragraph.

28. The quotation and many of the details in the paragraph come from Graves.

29. Hillman, "Puer and Senex," 17–18, notes that the *puer* archetype is often linked to child exposure.

30. In this she is like that serpent of old Nile who, obliquely reflected in the dialogue of a drunkard at another feast in *Antony and Cleopatra*, "is shap'd, sir, like itself . . . moves with it own organs . . . [and] lives by that which nourisheth it" (in the Arden Shakespeare, ed. M. R. Ridley, 2.7.41–45).

31. Here I differ decisively from the opinion of J. H. P. Pafford (lxxvii) that Perdita is less intelligent in the "debate" with Polixenes than stubborn in a peasant way.

32. Spenser's admirable female knight, Britomart, has often fallen under the censure of male readers who do not seem to see that her "irritability" results from the need to exercise vigilance over a "virtue"—chastity—that will be lost forever in male eyes if it is once defeated.

33. Mary Daly in *Gyn/Ecology: The Metaethics of Radical Feminism* (Boston: Beacon, 1978) gives an outline, informed by passionate outrage, of the injustices imposed on women by men in many cultures under the rationale of witchcraft.

Chapter Five

1. Unlike the others, it observes the classical unities of time, place, and action.

2. See Frank Kermode's extended discussion of this literature in his Introduction to *The Tempest,* the Arden Shakespeare (London: Methuen, 1954). All quotations from *The Tempest,* in parentheses in text, are drawn from this edition.

3. Nicholls, in the early chapters of *Chemical Theatre,* discusses the currency of such texts in Shakespeare's England and demonstrates their importance to his plays.

4. The early critical texts here are G. Wilson Knight's *The Shakespearean Tempest* (London: Methuen, 1953) and E. M. W. Tillyard's *The Elizabethan World Picture* (London: Chatto and Windus, 1943). Their leads have been followed by countless commentators since because what they outlined is basic to any full reading of the plays.

5. The phrase "implicate order" is taken from David Bohm's *Wholeness and the Implicate Order* (London: Routledge & Kegan Paul, 1983). It points to the theories of modern physics that have (re)discovered replications of pattern on small and

large scales throughout the universe—theories in harmony with beliefs prevailing in Shakespeare's time about microcosm, body politic, and macrocosm.

6. As close in time as 1608, death had been advocated for witches, especially white, or "blessing," witches who posed dangers greater than "damnifying sorcerers," who were less likely to lead the good Christian astray. See Christina Hole, *Witchcraft in England* (London: Collier-Macmillan, 1966), 130.

7. See chapter 1; for a fuller treatment, see my *Plato Baptized,* chap. 5.

8. Richard Niebuhr describes, in *Christ and Culture* (New York: Harper, 1951), the procession of such debates through two millennia and the range of positions taken by participants.

9. See Nicholl, *Chemical Theatre,* for one of the best accounts available of the art of the alchemist in Renaissance theory and practice, especially in relation to Shakespeare and his fellow dramatists.

10. Arden edition, xxxiv–xxxviii.

11. For an account of the wild man or Vice, see Rossiter, *English Drama from Early Times to the Elizabethans,* chaps. 1–3.

12. See Kermode, Introduction, xl, and note to 1.2.321–22.

13. *"In illo tempore"* is the phrase Eliade, *Cosmos and History,* uses to designate the lost harmony Freudians relate to separation from the mother. Rosemary Radford Reuther, "The Development of My Theology," *Religious Studies Review* 15, 1 (January 1989): 1–4, throws light on Caliban's story when she says that one "dimension of the ideology of domination is to claim that the dominated people 'sinned' in some aboriginal time, and thus their subjugation is justified as punishment."

14. The figure of Heathcliff, also characterized as a devil by those in *Wuthering Heights* who abuse him, presents similar issues in interpretation. I have always sensed Caliban in the literary ancestry of Bronte's monster.

15. See, for a recent instance, Paul Brown, " 'This thing of darkness I acknowledge Mine': *The Tempest* and the Discourse of Colonialism," in *Political Shakespeare,* ed. Jonathan Dollimore and Alan Sinfield (Manchester: Manchester University Press, 1985).

16. Archetypally, the configuration of the innocent maiden and the brute resembles that of Beauty and the Beast, or the Virgin and the Unicorn. Such patterns point to a needed psychic reintegration of the ideal or spiritual with the animal body.

17. For a more extended discussion, see the section on Plato's *Timaeus* in my *Plato Baptized,* chap. 2.

18. *A Midsummer Night's Dream,* ed. Harold F. Brooks, the Arden Shakespeare (London: Methuen, 1979), 4.1.199–217.

19. This work was popular in Elizabeth's England in the translation of William Adlington, 1566.

20. See the footnote to the passage in the Arden edition.

21. See chapter 1.

22. The male alienated by the thrust of *puer* idealism from more negative males dominated by the power principle must be integrated with his own feminine

principle, symbolized in the narrative by his daughter, before the reconciliation that depends on balance in the participating selves is possible.

23. Von Franz deals with this function of the anima in *On Divination and Synchronicity* (Toronto: Inner City Books, 1980), 110.

24. As Pericles eventually learns to name his lost Thaisa, his erstwhile consort-possession.

25. As Anthony Dawson sees it in *Shakespeare and the Art of Illusion* (Toronto: University of Toronto Press, 1978), 160.

26. It also echoes the reactions of many heroes in classical and Renaissance texts. See the footnote in the Arden edition, 37.

27. See Dawson, *Shakespeare and the Art of Illusion,* chap. 8.

28. For elaboration, see my discussion of Aristotle in *Plato Baptized,* 55–59.

29. Stephen Wall's review in the *Times Literary Supplement,* 10–16 June 1988, 649, of a performance by the National Theatre Company makes a similar observation about Prospero. The words in quotation are his.

30. Dawson, whose argument leads along paths totally different from mine, deals with the relation of Prospero to the *senex* as conventional comic figure in drama. See his *Shakespeare and the Art of Illusion,* p. 160.

31. This paragraph throughout owes debts to Hillman's classic study, "Senex and Puer." It quotes or paraphrases especially 16–17, 20–21.

32. One of the standard tricks of magicians in Renaissance fiction was the creation of an illusory body, perhaps of air as in *The Faerie Queene,* 1.1.45, to materialize an otherwise invisible spirit (Edmund Spenser, *Works,* ed. J. C. Smith and E. de Selincourt [Oxford University Press, 1910–11]).

33. Hillman, "Senex and Puer," 43–49.

34. Ibid., 45–46.

35. Here I am remembering Hillman's call for a psychology of soul as he presents it in *Re-visioning Psychology* (New York: Harper & Row, 1975) and his essay "On the Necessity of Abnormal Psychology," in *Facing the Gods* (Dallas: Spring Publications, 1980). But I am remembering even more the visionary psychology of Plotinus, which I outline in *Plato Baptized,* chap. 4.

36. Even in the story of one perfect human life, Christ cannot escape human struggle because he has taken on the full humanity that guarantees it.

37. I am describing the same performance (at Stratford, Ontario, in the late 1950s) that held my ten-year-old daughter and her classmates spellbound.

38. There may be an oblique encouragement to the audience to repeat their experience another day, but same time, same theater.

39. A current critical tendency to group *Henry VIII* with the Romances rather than the history plays bears out the observation on the nature of the genre: *The Tempest* may be the last of the Romances—or it may not. It all depends. See also Patricia Parker, *Inescapable Romance* (Princeton: Princeton University Press, 1979).

Chapter Six

1. The quoted phrases are from Shakespeare's Sonnet 18 (line 13) and 63 (lines 10 and 13). The sonnets may be consulted in any of the complete works cited in the Bibliography.

2. More detailed information on stage and critical history is available in the introductions to the Arden editions of the plays. For this chapter, I have also consulted reviews of recent performances in *Shakespeare Quarterly.*

Selected Bibliography

PRIMARY WORKS

The following, the first published texts of the Romances, are the ones followed by most modern editors. The First Quarto of *Pericles,* the only surviving text, is badly garbled. The other three texts, first published in the Folio of 1623, are of good quality.

Pericles, Prince of Tyre. First Quarto, 1609.
The Tragedie of Cymbeline. First Folio, 1623.
The Winter's Tale. First Folio, 1623.
The Tempest. First Folio, 1623.

Reliable modern editions follow. New Arden texts, listed first, are the ones used for reference in this book. Their introductions are extensive and reliable on textual and scholarly matters. Hoeniger's and Kermode's remain among the best critical treatments available; Nosworthy and Pafford are also well worth consulting. Collected editions are grouped last.

Hoeniger, F. D., ed. *Pericles.* The Arden Shakespeare. London: Methuen, 1963.
Nosworthy, J. M., ed. *Cymbeline.* The Arden Shakespeare. London: Methuen, 1955.
Pafford, J. H. P., ed. *The Winter's Tale.* Arden Shakespeare. London: Methuen, 1955.
Kermode, Frank, ed. *The Tempest.* Arden Shakespeare. London: Methuen, 1954.
Maxwell, J. C., ed. *Pericles.* Cambridge: Cambridge University Press, 1956. Introduction complements Hoeniger's on thorny textual problems.
Orgel, Stephen, ed. *The Tempest.* New Oxford Shakespeare Series. Clarendon Press, 1987.

Allen, Michael J., and Kenneth Muir, eds. *Shakespeare's Plays in Quarto: A Facsimile Edition of Copies Primarily from the Henry E. Huntington Library.* Berkeley and Los Angeles: University of California Press, 1982.
Bevington, David, ed. *The Complete Works of Shakespeare.* 3d ed. Glenview, Ill.: Scott Foresman & Co., 1980.

Evans, G. Blakemore, et al., eds. *The Riverside Shakespeare*. 2 vols. Boston: Houghton Mifflin, 1974.

Harbage, Alfred, gen. ed. *William Shakespeare: The Complete Works*. Pelican text rev. New York: Viking Press, 1977.

Hinman, Charlton, ed. *Norton Facsimile: The First Folio of Shakespeare*. New York: W. W. Norton, 1968.

Wells, Stanley, and Gary Taylor, eds. *William Shakespeare: The Complete Works*. Original spelling ed. Oxford: Oxford University Press, 1987.

SECONDARY WORKS

Books

Bergeron, David. *Shakespeare's Romances and the Royal Family*. Lawrence: University Press of Kansas, 1985. Discusses historical parallels to the family of James I in the Romances as re-presentations of the royal "text."

Bieman, Elizabeth. *Plato Baptized: Towards the Interpretation of Spenser's Mimetic Fictions*. Toronto: University of Toronto Press, 1988. Explains critical perspectives affecting this book more fully and technically than the present introduction. Also provides a fuller account of the Neoplatonic and biblical traditions informing the Romances and other Renaissance literature than can be given here.

Bohm, David. *Wholeness and the Implicate Order*. London: Routledge & Kegan Paul, 1980, 1983. A scientist's account of the primacy of order and pattern in the universe. Of interest to literary readers for the parallels it offers to microcosmic-macrocosmic thinking in the Renaissance.

Butler, E. M. *The Myth of the Magus*. Cambridge: Cambridge University Press, 1948. A classic study of ancient magic and later European mages, including John Dee.

Cobb, Noel. *Prospero's Island: The Secret Alchemy at the Heart of The Tempest*. London: Coventure, 1984. Stimulating but unidimensional tracing, by a Jungian analyst, of Prospero's transformation in terms of Renaissance alchemy.

Corrigan, Robert W., ed. *Comedy: Meaning and Form*. San Francisco: Chandler, 1965. A collection of articles, many of which illuminate the forms and effects of the Romances. See especially those by Christopher Fry, Nathan A. Scott, Jr., Susanne Langer, and C. L. Barber.

Curtius, E. R. *European Literature and the Latin Middle Ages*. Translated by Willard R. Trask. Bollingen series. Princeton: Princeton University Press, 1973, 98–101. An invaluable reference tool that traces topics and symbols still important in Shakespeare's time back to their classical and medieval roots.

Daly, Mary. *Gyn/Ecology: The Metaethics of Radical Feminism*. Boston: Beacon

Press, 1978. An angry book cataloging the injustices of men toward women in many cultures.

Davies, Stevie. *The Idea of Woman in Renaissance Literature: The Feminine Reclaimed.* Brighton: Harvester, 1986. Scholarly overview of Renaissance thinking from an optimistic, feminist, and Jungian perspective. Shakespeare chapters focus on the Romances.

Dawson, Anthony B. *Shakespeare and the Art of Illusion.* Toronto: University of Toronto Press, 1978. Works in later chapters with the merging of art and nature in *The Winter's Tale* and *The Tempest* and the merging of theatrical illusions with "real life" at the end of *The Tempest.*

Donne, John. "An Anatomy of the World: The First Anniversary." In *John Donne: The Complete English Poems.* Edited by A. J. Smith. Harmondsworth: Penguin, 1971. Illustrates the dark and fearful perspective on the world provoked by the new science at the time of the Romances.

Dusinberre, Juliet. *Shakespeare and the Nature of Women.* London: Macmillan, 1975. Finds that Shakespeare's treatment of women reflects a social change for the better stemming from Puritan influences and that he also furthers the process of change for the better.

Eliade, Mircea. *Cosmos and History: The Myth of the Eternal Return.* New York: Harper, 1958. Study in comparative mythology demonstrating patterns in ritual and consciousness that apply in literature and drama.

Felperin, Howard. *Shakespearean Romance.* Princeton: Princeton University Press, 1972. Places the Romances, including *Henry VIII,* within the romance mode and contexts of Elizabethan romance and Shakespeare's comedies and problem plays. Finds the Romances more problematic than earlier plays.

French, Marilyn. *Shakespeare's Division of Experience.* New York: Summit Books, 1981. Finds male characters in the Romances being taught the limits of power and the female characters often exiled: "that which is precluded from active power can manifest its power only by its absence."

French, Peter. *John Dee: the World of an Elizabethan Magus.* London: Routledge & Kegan Paul, 1972. Biography of the white magician who may have been a model for Prospero.

Freud, Sigmund. *Complete Psychological Works.* London: Hogarth Press, 1955. Vol. 17. A study of the psychological effects that follow when familiar (and familial) matters (like incest) that "ought to have remained . . . hidden . . . come to light." Especially pertinent to the grotesque elements in the Romances.

Frosh, Stephen. *The Politics of Psychoanalysis: An Introduction to Freudian and Post-Freudian Theory.* New Haven: Yale University Press, 1987. Outlines the history and explains the concepts of leading psychoanalysts.

Frye, Northrop. *A Natural Perspective: The Development of Shakespearean Comedy and Romance.* New York: Columbia, University Press 1965. Finds the Romances unified by recurring motifs and concerns: the relationship between audience and dramatic participants; the anchoring of myth in nature; triumph through time; the baptismal function of the sea.

Gadamer, Hans-Georg. *Truth and Method.* New York: Crossroads, 1985. (In German *Wahrheit und Methode,* 1960). An enormous work, rooted in Gadamer's grasp of Platonic and German philosophy. His theories of hermeneusis, emphasizing both the slipperiness of language and the possibilities of growth in understanding through grasping evanescent meanings, fit and inform the critical perspective of this book.

Goldberg, Jonathan. *James I and the Politics of Literature.* Baltimore: Johns Hopkins University Press, 1983. Studies "authority" and its "representations" in the period of the Romances—implying variously in "representations" historical figures, their political utterances, and literary texts addressed to court audiences. Little directly on the Romances but a strong supplement to the historical studies of Bergeron and Yates.

Graves, Robert. *The Greek Myths.* Harmondsworth: Penguin, 1955, rev. 1960. A two-volume compendium of classical myth drawn and summarized from ancient sources, usefully indexed.

Harding, M. Esther. *Woman's Mysteries.* New York: Harper & Row, 1971. An application of Jung's thinking to women's psychological experiences. Seminal on "the virgin" as an image of autonomous strength.

Hartwig, Joan. *Shakespeare's Tragicomic Vision.* Baton Rouge: Louisiana State University Press, 1972. Dealing with the plays' genre as tragicomedy, provides balance to works that read them as "romance." Chapters on each of four, with appendixes on authorship of *Pericles* and on *Henry VIII* and *Two Noble Kinsmen.*

Hillman, James. "On the Necessity of Abnormal Psychology: Ananke and Athene." In *Facing the Gods.* Edited by James Hillman. Dallas: Spring Publications, 1980. Insights on *ananke* applicable to Caliban and to many facets of other male characters: Pericles' depression, Posthumus's and Leontes' rages, Posthumus's "beating brain." Treats "pathology," or psychic disturbance, as a necessary step toward *metanoia* (baptism, transformation).

———. *Re-Visioning Psychology.* New York: Harper & Row, 1975. Treatment of "pathology" as road to divine insight, fuller than the previous article. Sections on Neoplatonic thinking in Hellenistic and Renaissance periods.

———. "Senex and Puer." In *Puer Papers.* Edited by James Hillman. Irving, Texas: Spring Publications, 1979. Extends the work of Jung and von Franz on "the *puer*" into the *puer-senex* archetype that remains troublesome within the individual psyche as long as the poles are separate from each other. Pertinent to male protagonists in all four Romances.

Hole, Christina. *Witchcraft in England.* London: Collier-Macmillan, 1966. Brief survey of witchcraft and magic in England, popular in style but generally reliable.

Jardine, Lisa. *Still Harping on Daughters.* Brighton: Harvester Press, 1983. Historical and feminist. Includes sections on Elizabethan eroticism, "the speech of strong women," and "the saving stereotype of female heroism."

Jung, Carl Gustav. *Memories, Dreams, Reflections.* Edited by Aniela Jaffe. Translated by Richard and Clara Winston. London: Collins and Routledge & Kegan Paul, 1964. Chapters on Freud and on "confrontations with the Unconscious" useful to place Jung in the spectrum of modern analytical disciplines.

_____. *Modern Man in Search of a Soul.* New York: Harcourt Brace & World, 1933. A brief and central document that is another good introduction to Jungian thinking.

_____. *C. G. Jung Speaking.* Edited by William McGuire and R. F. C. Hull. London: Pan, Picador, 1980. Collected documents offering other entrées to Jung's thinking.

Kahn, Coppélia. "The Providential Tempest and the Shakespearean Family." In *Representing Shakespeare.* Edited by Murray M. Schwartz and Kahn. Baltimore: Johns Hopkins University Press, 1980. Sees the Romances, more oedipally oriented than the comedies, dealing with the freeing of sexuality from the threat of degradation. Primarily Freudian; interested in doubles and the uncanny.

Kernan, Alvin B. *The Playwright as Magician: Shakespeare's Image of the Poet in the English Public Theatre.* New Haven: Yale University Press, 1979. Throughout, Kernan deals with the paradoxical tension between the views of art as illusion and art as high vision. See especially chapters covering *The Tempest* and "The Playwright as Magician."

Knight, G. Wilson. *The Shakespearean Tempest with a Chart of Shakespeare's Dramatic Universe.* London: Methuen, 1953. Basic to subsequent discussions of Shakespeare's use of storm images to represent chaos and music to represent harmonious order in the universe.

Kristeva, Julia. *Tales of Love.* Translated by Leon S. Roudiez. New York: Columbia University Press, 1987. Chapter on *Romeo and Juliet* treats love as "the utopic wager that paradise lost can be made lasting." Post-Freudian perspective on love relationships in the context of the lost unity between mother and child. (The Romances do not enter the discussion directly.)

Lenz, Carolyn Ruth Swift, Gayle Greene, and Carol Thomas Neely, eds. *The Woman's Part: Feminist Criticism of Shakespeare.* Urbana: University of Illinois Press, 1980. A range of feminist approaches to Shakespeare. One article only on the Romances (by Lorrie Jerrell Leininger) links Miranda to the Princess Elizabeth, daughter of James I.

Lewis, C. S. *The Discarded Image: An Introduction to Medieval and Renaissance Literature.* Cambridge: Cambridge University Press, 1964. A clear description of Renaissance thinking on the order of the universe, as it is derived from classical texts.

McFarland, Thomas. *Shakespeare's Pastoral Comedy.* Chapel Hill: University of North Carolina Press, 1972. Good on the interrelationships of comedy, pastoral and the Romances and on the Platonic tradition. Readings of *The Winter's Tale* and *The Tempest* build on traditional materials.

Neumann, Erich. *Art and the Creative Unconscious.* New York: Harper & Row, 1966. The standard Jungian work on "participation mystique."

————.*The Great Mother.* New York: Bollingen, 1955, Pantheon, 1963. Investigates the archetype through ancient myth, arguing the importance of "the mother" in the development of the male psyche.

Nicholl, Charles. *The Chemical Theatre.* London: Routledge & Kegan Paul, 1980. Traces the history of English alchemy in relation to literature and drama and demonstrates its pervasive presence in *King Lear.* One of the best and clearest accounts of alchemy available for literary purposes.

Novy, Marianna L. *Love's Argument: Gender Relations in Shakespeare.* Chapel Hill: University of North Carolina Press, 1984. Deals with two related but distinct gender conflicts in Shakespeare: between mutuality and patriarchy and between emotion and control.

Nuttall, A. D. *A New Mimesis: Shakespeare and the Representation of Reality.* London: Methuen, 1983. Provocative and sane arguments for the conviction that characters in literature are more than mere formal elements, that even "unrealistic" literature is "not insulated from this varying world."

Parker, Patricia. *Inescapable Romance: The Poetics of a Mode.* Princeton: Princeton University Press, 1979. Exciting overview of romance in many periods. Emphasizes the inevitability of open endings in the genre.

Parker, Patricia, and Geoffrey Hartman, eds. *Shakespeare and the Question of Theory.* London: Methuen, 1975. Excellent articles in which to study current trends in Shakespeare criticism. Not much directly on the Romances.

Perkins, William. *The Works of William Perkins.* Introduced and edited by Ian Breward. Appleford: Sutton-Courtenay Press, 1970. Moderate Calvinist theology from Shakespeare's England. Provides the basis for an understanding of the plays' use of "baptism" in the sea as a metaphor for transformation in the soul.

Peterson, Douglas L. *Time, Tide and Tempest: A Study of Shakespeare's Romances.* San Marino: Huntington Library, 1973. Traces in the romances a shift in Shakespeare's focus "from the destructive power of evil to the restorative power of good" and finds the four plays "affirming . . . a morally coherent universe" sustained by the force of love.

Plato: The Collected Dialogues, including the Letters. Edited by Edith Hamilton and Huntington Cairns. Princeton: Princeton University Press, 1961, 1973. Accessible translations by various hands. Comprehensive topical index helps orient a beginner to Platonic thinking.

Polanyi, Michael. *Personal Knowledge: Towards a Post-Critical Philosophy.* Chicago: University of Chicago Press, 1968. Theory on ways of knowing, tacit and focal, based in Polanyi's experience as a scientist. Important to theories developed in *Plato Baptized* and implied in this book.

Righter, Anne. *Shakespeare and the Idea of the Play.* London: Chatto and Windus, 1964. Clear introduction to the history of drama leading up to Shakespeare. Final chapter on the Romances explores the image of the play and the function of the play within the play.

Rossiter, A. P. *English Drama from Early Times to the Elizabethans.* London: Hutchinson University Library, 1950. Like Righter, an excellent introduction to the dramatic history that shaped Shakespeare.

Samuels, Andrew. *Jung and the Post-Jungians.* London: Routledge & Kegan Paul, 1985. A map of the world of depth psychology, tracing Jung's differences from Freud and the differences emerging among those shaped by the thinking of both.

Stone, Lawrence. *The Family, Sex and Marriage in England, 1500–1800.* London: Weidenfield and Nicolson, 1977. Social history demonstrating the danger of taking present assumptions on family life back to the plays uncritically.

Tillyard, E. M. W. *The Elizabethan World Picture.* London: Chatto & Windus, 1943. Clear description of three aspects of Renaissance thinking: the chain, the corresponding planes of reality, and the cosmic dance. Still useful for a beginner able to allow for its overschematic nature.

_____. *Shakespeare's Last Plays.* London: Chatto and Windus, 1938. Brief introduction to three of the Romances, omitting *Pericles;* still useful on the milieu of Elizabethan romance and on the patterns of tragedy in relation to the Romances.

Traister, Barbara Howard. *Heavenly Necromancers: The Magician in English Renaissance Drama.* Columbia: University of Missouri Press, 1984. Useful background and descriptions of the stereotypical magician; chapter on Prospero.

Uphaus, Robert W. *Beyond Tragedy: Structure and Experience in Shakespeare's Romances.* Lexington: University Press of Kentucky, 1981. Concerned with emotional and experiential responses to the Romances. Sees the "new starts" I call "baptisms" or "transformations" as all important. Chapter on *Henry VIII* extending Romance into history.

von Franz, Marie Louise. *On Divination and Synchronicity: The Psychology of Meaningful Chance.* Toronto: Inner City Books, 1980. Relates many of the archetypes, including the virgin, to Jung's thinking.

_____. *Puer Aeternus.* Santa Monica: Sigo Press, 1981. Classical study of the *puer* figure in Jung's thinking, applying it to figures from modern European literature.

Walker, D. P. *Spiritual and Demonic Magic from Ficino to Campanella.* Notre Dame: University of Notre Dame Press, 1975 (reprint of Warburg Institute, 1958). Historical study of magic in Renaissance Europe, illuminating the magic in the plays.

Wallis, R. T. *Neoplatonism.* London: Duckworth, 1972. Detailed survey of the ancient Neoplatonists, with useful chapter on their subsequent influence.

Warner, Marina. *Alone of All Her Sex.* New York: Alfred A. Knopf, 1976. Traces the cult of the Virgin Mary through history and finds it an expression of "the Platonic yearning towards the ideal." Discusses Mary as virgin, queen, bride, mother, and intercessor.

Woodman, David. *White Magic and English Renaissance Drama.* Cranbury, N.J.: Associated University Presses, 1971. Relates the white magician to alchemy, Neoplatonic philosophy, herbal lore, and Renaissance church history. Chapters on healers in Shakespeare and on Prospero.

Woodman, Marion. *The Pregnant Virgin: A Process of Psychological Transformation.* Toronto: Inner City Books, 1985. Finds that a woman must undergo initiation into her body and the world of matter, experiencing matter as anima, before she can enjoy in "the inner virgin" full consciousness of self. Especially pertinent to Imogen's initiation.

Yates, Frances. *Shakespeare's Last Plays: A New Approach.* London: Routledge and Kegan Paul, 1975. Finds the children of James I, Princess Elizabeth and Prince Henry, keys to interpreting much in *Cymbeline* and *The Tempest*.

――――. *Theatre of the World.* Chicago: University Of Chicago Press, 1969. Relates Renaissance magic (through Dr. John Dee) to the history of stage design in London, and to the masque.

Articles on Individual Romances

Pericles

Dickey, Stephen. "Language and Role in *Pericles*." *English Literary Renaissance* 16 (1986): 550–66. Argues that the appearance of "complex self-conciousness" in Pericles and Gower, and a depth unexpected in the genre, is achieved through language suggesting role playing in both characters.

Gorfain, Phyllis. "Puzzle and Artifice: The Riddle as Metapoetry in *Pericles*." *Shakespeare Survey* 29 (1976):11–20. Exploration of structural parallels involving riddling, the choruses, and dumb shows. Finds these metatheatrical devices pointing to the transformative power of illusion.

Hillman, Richard. "Shakespeare's Gower and Gower's Shakespeare: The Larger Debt of *Pericles*." *Shakespeare Quarterly* 36 (1987):227–40. Finds the figure of Gower in *Pericles* "the most sustained literary illusion in Shakespeare," a representation of Shakespeare's inspiration, and a sign for the transforming power of poetry.

Cymbeline

Hoeniger, F. D. "Irony and Romance in *Cymbeline*." *Studies in English Literature*

11 (1962):219–28. Suggests the interpreter must adopt the perspectives of both irony and romance for a full understanding.

Landry, D. E. "Dream as History: The Strange Unity of *Cymbeline*." *Shakespeare Quarterly* 3 (1982):68–79. Roots the play's "unusually primitive" dramaturgical effects in Imogen's and Posthumus's dreams and finds it sophisticatedly "aware of its own artifice."

Moffet, Robin. "*Cymbeline* and the Nativity." *Shakespeare Quarterly* 13 (1962): 207–18. Illuminates the play's form and many of its details through Holinshed's note that "Kymbeline" reigned when "Christ Ieusus our saviour was borne, all nations content to obeie the Romane emperours."

Turner, Robert Y. "Slander in *Cymbeline* and Other Jacobean Tragicomedies." *English Literary History* 13 (1983):182–202. Sees the speech of "dispraisers" like Iachimo and Cloten in reaction to contemporary literary and dramatic satire, and set to question "any outlook that fails to allow for the exceptional."

The Winter's Tale

Felperin, Howard. "Tongue-tied our queen? The Deconstruction of Presence in *The Winter's Tale*." In *Shakespeare and the Question of Theory*, 3–18. Edited by Patricia Parker and Geoffrey Hartman. New York: Methuen, 1985. Excellent demonstration and discussion of slippery language in *The Winter's Tale*.

Gourlay, Patricia Southard. "'O my most sacred lady': Female Metaphor in *The Winter's Tale*." *English Literary Renaissance* 5 (1975):375–95. Arguing that the Neoplatonic Venus lies behind both figures, finds both Hermione's and Paulina's "femaleness" revealing the "limitations of a masculine world."

Neely, Carol Thomas. "*The Winter's Tale*: The Triumph of Speech." *Studies in English Literature* 15 (1966):321–38. Defends the langauge of the play against critical detraction by demonstrating "speech" as both "means" and "mark" of the dynamic of restoration.

The Tempest

Brown, Paul. "'This thing of darkness I acknowledge mine': *The Tempest* and the Discourse of Colonialism." In *Political Shakespeare*. Edited by Jonathan Dollimore and Alan Sinfield. Manchester: Manchester University Press, 1985. Finds Caliban typifying New World victims of the Europeans and *The Tempest* radically ambiguous on the matter of contemporary colonization.

Mowat, Barbara A. "Prospero, Agrippa, and Hocus Pocus." *English Literary Renaissance* 11 (1981):281–303. Points to elements in Prospero's magic that are more frivolous and stagey than serious, moral, or "supernatural" as evidence that *The Tempest* is, among other things, about stage illusion.

McNamara, Kevin R. "Golden Worlds at Court: *The Tempest* and Its Masque." *Shakespeare Studies* 19 (1987):183–202. Taking Prospero's wedding masque as the dramatic center of the play, speculates on what the Jacobean audience would have seen in performance.

Pierce, Robert B. "'Very Like a Whale': Scepticism and Seeing in *The Tempest*." *Shakespeare Survey* 38 (1985):167–73. Sees in *The Tempest*'s perplexed and perplexing characters the expression of a playful and wise skepticism.

Index

N.B.: 1. Books, wherever practicable, are cited under author.
2. Entries for the Notes and References section will cite authors who are included in the Annotated Bibliography only when additional information needs to be indicated.